I0148785

Back to Sherlock Holmes

Literary Studies in
Sherlock Holmes Stories

A selection of other books by Yair Mazor:

Hounding the Hound of the Baskervilles
A Poetic Portrait of the Detective Novel

Poetic Acrobat:
The Poetry of Ronny Someck

Nocturnal Lament:
The Poetry of David Fogel and Modern Hebrew Poetry

Broken Twig:
The Poetry of Dalia Ravikovich and Modern Hebrew Poetry

Bridled Bird:
The Poetry of Nathan Zach and Modern Hebrew Poetry

The Flower and the Fury:
The Poetry of Yonah Wollach and Modern Hebrew Poetry

Who Wrought the Bible? Unveiling the Bible's Aesthetic Secrets

Israeli Poetry of the Holocaust

Somber Lust: The Art of Amos Oz

Pain, Pining, and Pine Trees: Contemporary Hebrew Poetry

The Triple Cord: Agnon, Hamsun, Strindberg:
Where Hebrew and Scandinavian Meet

The Poetry of Asher Reich: Portrait of a Hebrew Poet

The Hidden Bible
Unearthing the Bible's Artistic Secrets: Essays on Biblical Literature

Back to Sherlock Holmes

Literary Studies in
Sherlock Holmes Stories

YAIR MAZOR

HenschelHAUS Publishing, Inc.
Milwaukee, Wisconsin

Copyright © 2020 by the University of Wisconsin-Milwaukee
All right reserved.

Published by
HenschelHAUS Publishing, Inc.
www.henschelHAUSbooks.com

ISBN: 978159598-699-3
E-ISBN:978159598-700-6
LCCN: 2019930270

This book is dedicated to:
my beloved brother, Professor Nimrod Moiseyev;
my beloved sister-in-law, Dr. Esther Moiseyev;
my beloved daughter, Dr. Yael Mazor;
and my beloved niece, attorney Chamutal Beno.
All of them are wrapped by my love.

~ ~ ~ ~ ~

"You have heard about me, Mr. Holmes," she cried, "else how could you know all that?"

"Never mind," said Holmes laughingly. "It is my business to know things. Perhaps I have trained myself to see what others overlook."

—Sherlock Holmes in *A Case of Identity*

CONTENTS

INTRODUCTION:
MAPPING THE POETIC PORTRAIT OF DETECTIVE LITERATURE

Gotthold Ephraim Lessing, in his book, *Laocoon: An Essay on the Limits of Painting and Poetry*, makes a distinction between two kinds of art: spatial art and temporal art. In each of these genres, the artistic medium determines the reception of the product by the target audience. In spatial art (painting, sculpture), the artistic product is grasped in space, in the blink of an eye, not as a continuum or progression over time. An instant is usually sufficient to discern the details of the painting or the sculpture, in order for them to be grasped by the beholder in the space where the artwork is presented. Temporal art, on the other hand (literature, dance, music), requires a length of time to absorb it (about two hours for music or dance, long hours, sometimes weeks, for fiction) in order to take it in, appreciate it, and internalize its content, significance, and impact.

The medium of time dictates a certain dynamic in the process of absorbing an artistic work. In literature, this dynamic dictates the way in which the verbal elements (words, sentences, paragraphs, chapters) are distributed along the continuum of the text. Thus, information placed at a later stage on the textual continuity impacts and determines the way the reader processes and understands

1

that information. This phenomenon is discernable in the literary device known as *enjambment* (run-on line) common in poetry: when the line is not long enough to contain the syntactic unit, the sentence "runs" onto the subsequent line. This can occur over several lines.

There are three types of enjambment: One, in which later information is added to earlier information without effecting any change in the understanding or interpretation of that information. Take, for instance, the run-on lines from two poems by the Hebrew poet Yehuda Amichai:

> *"Our lives depend more on*
> *Words....*

> *"I saw an erased life*
> *Like a letter in the rain..."*

The later information (in the second lines) does not alter our understanding of the previous line; it modifies, refines, and enhances it.

In the second type of enjambment, the later information significantly changes the way in which the earlier information was understood, but does not alter it completely. Here is an example from another poem by Yehuda Amichai:

> *"The white sand*
> *Is an ideal heavenly material."*

The first line (earlier information) is rather bland and does not carry much significance. However, the later information in the second line throws new light and invests the earlier line with new original meaning. The white sand is an ideal heavenly material, a reference to God's promise to Abraham that his descendants will be as numerous as the sand on the seashore.

In the third type of enjambment, the later information totally changes the way the earlier information has been understood; it forces the reader to go back and re-read the earlier line and re-interpret it. Here is another example from a poem by Yehuda Amichai:

> *"My beloved wears a long white dress*
> *Of sleep."*

The first line (earlier information) evokes a positive impression, an allusion to a pure, innocent bride. However, the additional information in the next line ("Of sleep") undoes or reverses the earlier interpretation: sleep is a common metaphor for death, and the white dress is no longer the bridal attire but a burial garment.

Consider this example from another Hebrew poet, Nathan Zach:

> *"Othello bent over Desdemona to put an end*
> *To the play."*

While the first line (earlier information) evokes thoughts of tragedy through the reference to Shakespeare's *Othello*, the next line (later information) turns the tragedy into a comedy. Othello is no longer the familiar tragic hero, but only an actor playing Othello, who for some reason decides to end the play earlier than expected (perhaps he has tickets to a ball game or is simply tired of playing the same role night after night). The enjambment renders the reading of the lines more dynamic, vital, and exciting.

In a prose text such as a novel, the dynamics of continuous text occur over bigger textual chunks, such as paragraphs and chapters.

In fact, there is only one difference between prose and poetry: in a poem, the poet decides the length of the lines for poetic reasons (as in the case of enjambment), while in prose, the publisher decides the length of lines, for technical-economical reasons, such as the format of the book and its ability to attract potential buyers.

In a prose work, there is a tension between the *fabula*, which is the sum total of events occurring along the textual continuum's chronological sequence, and the *syuzhet*, the organizational principle of the elements of the plot, which often disrupts and frustrates the chronological order of the *fabula*. (Both the terms *fabula* and *syuzhet* originated with Russian formalists.) To be sure, the deviation of the *syuzhet* from the chronological order of the *fabula* has an artistic, aesthetic motivation, and it affects and determines the understanding and interpretation of the text throughout the reading process.

In a detective story, the deviation of the *syuzhet* from the order of the *fabula* is drastic; the first event in the "fabula," the initial crime – its perpetrator and the motive – are postponed by the *syuzhet* until the last stage of the sequential plot. The essence of the detective story is dictated by the tension and by the conflict that exists between the *fabula* and the *syuzhet*. There is a constant clash between various elements along the textual continuum, a variance that turns the reading into a dynamic, vital, and exuberant process.

The reading process of a detective story resembles a pendulum constantly swinging in opposite directions. The text supplies information, which encourages and compels the reader to formulate a certain hypothesis regarding the mystery; that hypothesis will lead to solving the crime. However, along the way, new information is injected into the process, impelling the reader to discard the first hypothesis and adopt a new one in its stead. Thus, the reader oscillates between competing hypotheses, as new information is introduced, rendering the reading process more challenging and rewarding.

This dynamic reading process is a continuous course of "filling the gap." What is happening? Who does it? Why do they do it? These gaps oblige the reader to examine new pieces of information as they are added along the text while discarding old assumptions, coming to new conclusions that eventually lead to solving the mystery.

The reader is called upon to patiently and thoughtfully map and piece together the elements of the text and decide which of those elements are marginal and misleading and which are relevant and crucial. Thus, the reader of a detective story becomes a prominent collaborator in the plot.

This is how Austin Freeman puts it:

> *The problem having been stated, the data for its solution are presented inconspicuously and in a sequence purposely dislocated so as to conceal*

their connection; and the reader's task is to collect the data, to rearrange them in their correct, logical sequence and ascertain their relations, when the solution of the problem should at once become obvious. (1)

Freeman here formulates the principles, the articles of faith, which the detective story must follow. It is permissible, perhaps desirable, to put obstacles and hindrances on the reader's way to the solution, but it is definitely impermissible to intentionally mislead and deceive the reader. The text must lead readers to a point where all the facts needed to solve the mystery are at their disposal (even if some facts are presented indirectly or ambiguously). All that is left for the reader to do is arrange the facts in chronological, logical order and, independently, arrive at the conclusion that leads to the solution of the puzzle.

Freeman seems to be inspired by Aristotle's *Poetics* when he lays out the principles of the detective story:

The conclusion must emerge truly and inevitably from the premises: it must be the only possible conclusion, and must leave the competent reader in no doubt as to its unimpeachable truth. (2)

E. M. Wrong concurs that the reader must never be deceived or led astray. However, Wrong emphasizes the right of the author of the detective story to put obstacles along the reader's way to solving the mystery. (3)

Willard Wright underlines the most desirable pattern of the detective story:

Introduction

The truth must at all times be in the printed
word, so if the reader should go back over the
book, he would find that the solution had been
there all the time, if he had sufficient shrewd-
ness to grasp it. (4)

John Ball stresses the importance of "fair play" (between author and reader) that must exist in a detective story:

If the detective saw the object, the reader must
see it too and be given the same chance to apply
it as a clue to the solution of the mystery. (5)

And he adds later:

If the surprise of the solution depends on infor-
mation not offered to the reader, then the author
violated the form.

The skillful, attentive reader may find himself/herself in a race with the detective: who will be the first to solve the mystery. In some respects, the reader has an advantage over the detective, because the reader has access to linguistic material (such as analogies, metonyms, expressions, and idioms) that is not accessible to the detective.

S.S. Van Dine lists the rules of detective fiction:

* The culprit must be determined by logical
   deduction – not by accident or coincidence or
   unmotivated confession.

* The problem of the crime must be solved by strictly naturalistic means, not spiritualistic, metaphysical means that contravene logic.

* The culprit must turn out to be a person who has played a more or less prominent part in the story – that is, a person with whom the reader is familiar and in whom he has taken interest.

* The crime in a detective story must never turn out to be an accident or a suicide.

* The motives for all crimes in detective stories should be personal. International plotting and war politics belong in a different category of fiction, such as secret service tales.

Van Dine concludes:

If the reader, after learning the explanation for the crime, should reread the book, he should see that the solution had, in a sense, been staring him in the face – that all the clues really pointed to the culprit, and that if he had been as clever as the detective, he should have solved the mystery himself without going on to the final chapter.

Ellery Queen puts it somewhat similarly:

"At this point in the story, you [the reader] are in possession of all the facts needed to build up a complete and logical solution of the crime. You job is to spot the vital clues, assemble them in a rational order, and from them deduce the one

and only possible criminal. It can be done; it has been done, as you will see.

Ronald A. Knox adds an important principle:

"The detective must not himself commit the crime." (6)

Knox emphasizes that the reader must have access to the same reservoir of information that the detective has at his disposal. Since detective fiction is predicated on the *syuzhet* manipulating the order of the *fabula*, we can confidently say that composition is at the center of the detective story, composition being the organization of the textual sequence. Some scholars of detective fiction maintain that every thematic material embedded in the text must be directly relevant to the solving of the crime.

Based on this assertion, Nils Clausson, for instance, claims that Conan Doyle's *The Hound of the Baskervilles* should be classified as a Gothic novel rather than as a detective story. This claim, however, can be disproved, because all thematic material that contributes to the detective story without vitiating or detracting from the criminal mystery should be welcome, perhaps even required, in order to create milieu, ambience, and backdrop that can enrich the mystery and contribute to its veracity. The rationality of the criminal mystery certainly benefits from being anchored in a thematic milieu that supports and enriches it.

Some literary scholars wonder if detective fiction is "real" literature. This query is as relevant as wondering if a metal or plastic chair is as "real" as a wooden chair. Detective fiction is an independent, legitimate literary genre, just as ballads, epic poems, mythological, or lyrical poetry are various genres of poetry, and the historical novel or stream-of-consciousness novel are legitimate genres of prose writing.

Fiction is distinct from historical, scientific, or political writing in that the latter is written for the purpose of education, edification, and instruction, whereas fiction is written for the purpose of eliciting an emotional reaction from the reader (either attraction or aversion) or for bestowing intellectual pleasure, as detective literature does. A history book may use elaborate, colorful language and make a very good read, but it is not *belles lettres*, not literature, because its main purpose is to instruct and educate, not to elicit emotional reaction, and the emotional reaction derived from detective fiction is, in essence, intellectual. It does not seek to educate or to impart knowledge; it is on a par with novels by the likes of Dostoyevsky, Zola, or Tolstoy or, for that matter, with children's literature. Detective fiction forms part of a respectable, venerable aesthetic environment.

Sherlock Holmes's detective stories can be divided into three distinct categories, three sub-genres. Each Sherlock Holmes story is based on two basic principles: the detective element and the mystery element. The detective element is dictated by the investigation Sherlock Holmes conducts (and to some by extent the reader, too) into the mystery introduced at the beginning of the story (for the most part this is a murder or some other crime). *En route* to solving the mystery, the text is filled with clues and hints that allow the reader to gradually crack the case and solve the mystery.

The element of mystery is enhanced by atmospherics, by nocturnal descriptions of town and country, by foul, inclement weather; thick, all-enveloping fog; suffocating mist; and persistent rain.

Each sub-genre is determined by the interaction and the ratio between those two elements. In the first sub-genre, the detective pursuit is most prominent: Sherlock Holmes's detective procedural (as well as the reader's) takes center stage and occupies most of the action. The text is strewn with clues that enable the reader to take part in the detective process. The best example of this sub-genre is *The Hound of the Baskervilles*.

Despite the gloomy, mysterious atmosphere that envelops the book and invests it with a Gothic, melancholy mood, it is investigative, detective pursuit that is the dominant part and the mainstay of the action.

Some other stories belonging to the first sub-genre are *The Resident Patient, The Crooked Man, The Man with the Twisted Lip,* and *The Adventure of Six Napoleons.*

In the second sub-genre, the mysterious atmosphere is still accorded an important place, but the main difference from the first sub-genre is the detective investigation itself. Sherlock Holmes continues to pursue the criminals with dedication and vigor, but without supplying the reader with many clues. Holmes is the only one conducting the investigation, while the reader is shunned and excluded. Typical of this category are the stories *A Scandal in Bohemia* and *The Adventure of the Yellow Face.*

In the third sub-genre, the detective investigation is all but eliminated. Instead, mystery, atmosphere, ambience, and mood take center stage. Only toward the end of the story, when he sums up, in general terms, the nature of the crime committed, does Sherlock Holmes reclaim his place. Examples of this category are the stories *The Adventure of the Solitary Cyclist, The Adventure of the Beryl Coronet*, and *The Adventure of the Golden Pince-Nez.*

Notes

1) Austin Freeman, "The Art of the Detective Story," in Howard Haycraft , ed., *The Art of the Mystery Story.* Simon and Schuster, New York, 1946, p. 14.

2) Ibid.

3) E. M. Wrong, "Crime and Detection" in Howard Haycraft, ed. , *The Art of the Mystery Story*, Simon and Schuster, New York, 1946, Ibid.

4) Willard Wright, "The Great detective Stories" in Howard Haycraft, ed., *The Art of the Detective Story.* p. 40.

5. John Ball, "Murder at Large" in John Ball, ed., *The Mystery Story*, University of California San Diego Press, San Diego, p. 23.

6) Ronald A. Knox, "A Detective Story Decalogue" in Howard Haycraft, ed., *The Art of the Mystery Story*, p. 196.

MYSTERIES UNEARTHED: IN THE COMPANY OF SHERLOCK HOLMES

LEADING ASTRAY IS THE NAME OF THE GAME
THE STORY *SILVER BLAZE*

Sherlock Holmes tells Dr. Watson that he has to travel to Dartmoor, to King Pyland Stable, to investigate the disappearance of a favorite racehorse, Silver Blaze, and the murder of the horse's trainer. Two important points need to be made regarding the mystery of the horse and the murder of its trainer. The first has to do with the order of presentation of these two mysteries: first the horse's disappearance, then the murder mystery. This strange order will be repeated later. Normally, a murder case would trump a missing horse, but here the order is reversed.

Moreover, even at this early stage in the story, the reader is "convinced" that the trainer was indeed murdered. Only toward the conclusion of the story does it become apparent that there was no murder. Thus, the insistence on murder from the outset dupes the reader: he/she is trapped in an erroneous conception.

On the train ride to Dartmoor, Holmes, as is his wont, flaunts his mental acuity:

Our rate at present is fifty-three and a half miles
an hour—but the telegraph posts upon this line
are sixty yards apart, and the calculation is a
simple one."

Holmes proceeds to elaborate on one of the basic principles of his analytical rational method of deduction:

The difficulty is to detach the framework of fact –
of absolute, undeniable fact – from the embellish-
ments of theorists and reporters. Then, having
established ourselves upon this sound basis, it is
our duty to see what inference may be drawn
and what are the special points upon which the
whole mystery turns.

The deception begins with Holmes's comment, "... beyond the arrest of young Fitzroy Simpson, nothing had been done..." which piques our curiosity: Who is Simpson? Why was he arrested? What is going on? Opening this information gap creates tension and initiates the mystery plot.

A young, well-dressed man, looking visibly nervous, appears one night at King's Pyland Stables, where Silver Blaze, Colonel Ross's fastest horse, is kept. A stable boy wakes up John Straker, the trainer, who then goes out in the dark and never returns. His body is found in the morning. It is clear that he fought his assailant. In his right hand he holds a small, rather delicate knife, while in his left he clasps a cravat belonging to the stranger, Simpson. The stable boy, who was on duty the night before, is found in a stupor, apparently having been drugged by powdered opium that was put in his dinner. The stable boy continues to sleep for long hours.

Simpson, it transpires, is a well-mannered wealthy young man. He claims that he came to the stable the night before to obtain information about the competing horses. This is a rather implausible explanation. Why did he show up so late at night? What accounts for his nervous behavior? Why did he not come at a more reasonable hour? Was he attacked by the trainer, and did he kill him during the fight that ensued? After all, Simpson's cravat was found in the clenched hand of the dead trainer. Thus, the suspicion for the murder of the trainer falls on Simpson. His explanation for his anxious behavior the night before, near the stable of the famous horse, sounds unconvincing.

Holmes says:

> *We may leave the question of who killed John Straker for the instant, and confine ourselves to finding out what has become of the horse.*

This is an almost absurd inversion of actions, but as is often the case with Sherlock Holmes, even the strangest of his decisions is based on pure logic.

The convention of detective fiction—especially of Sherlock Holmes stories—dictates that the theories advanced by the police inspector are always disproved. Thus, Inspector Gregory states:

> *The net is drawn pretty close round Fitzroy Simpson,' he said, 'and I believe myself that he is our man.*

But this time the police detective evinces some caution, adding:

> *At the same time I recognize that the evidence is purely circumstantial, and that some new development may upset it.*

In other words, we have a pendulum movement indicating that Simpson may not be the culprit. But soon enough, the pendulum swings in the opposite direction, pointing to Simpson's guilt.

Dr. Watson says:

> *The evidence against him is certainly very strong. He had a great interest in the disappearance of the favorite. He lies under the suspicion of having poisoned the stable boy, he was undoubtedly out in the storm, he was armed with a heavy stick, and his cravat was found in the dead man's hand. I really think we have enough to go before a jury.*

But then, according to another convention of Sherlock Holmes stories, Dr. Watson, too, is always wrong. Holmes dismisses his theories, and thus the pendulum swings in the opposite direction again (acquitting Simpson of the crime):

> *Holmes shook his head, 'A clever counsel would tear it all to rags,' said he. "Why should he take the horse out of the stable? If he wished to injure*

it, why could he not do it there? Has a duplicate key been found in his possession? What chemist sold him the powdered opium? Above all, where could he, a stranger to the district, hide a horse, and such a horse as this?

The pendulum sways back and forth, first asserting Simpson's guilt then dismissing the suspicion against him.

Some clues suggesting that the (now dead) trainer Straker is the culprit are found among the objects in his pockets: five gold sovereigns, a silver watch with a gold chain, a candle (for what purpose?—To do something at night that cannot be done in daylight), and an ivory-handled knife with a very delicate inflexible blade.

Holmes comments, "This is a very singular knife." Dr. Watson confirms that such a knife is used for performing delicate surgery:

A very delicate blade devised for very delicate work. A strange thing for a man to carry with him upon a rough expedition, especially as it would not shut in his pocket.

The question arises: what was the trainer doing at night that required a candle and a delicate surgical knife?

Holmes further wonders about another item found in the trainer's pocket: a receipt for a fancy lady's dress. "Twenty-two guineas is rather heavy for a single costume," comments Holmes. This puts further suspicion on the horse trainer. Who is the woman for whom the dress was bought? Holmes poses the question about the luxury garment to the trainer's wife, who denies that her husband ever bought her such a dress. The conclusion: the trainer had a secret that had to do with another woman.

Holmes suggests changing the order of the investigation:

> *We may leave the question of who killed John*
> *Straker for the instant, and confine ourselves to*
> *finding out what has become of the horse.*

Holmes is convinced that the solution to the murder mystery is dependent on solving the mystery of the missing horse. Holmes does not comment on the suspicious objects in the dead trainer's pockets, but it is obvious that he is well aware of them.

Holmes and Watson track the horse's hooves in the moor to a competitor's stable in Mapleton. We noted earlier three swings of the pendulum regarding Simpson's guilt or innocence. When it sways toward exoneration, the plot takes another turn: focusing on the trainer and the incriminating objects found in his pockets. From here the course of the investigation tilts toward a new tack: finding the horse.

Holmes and Watson follow the horse and the man leading him (first there were only the horse's tracks, then human footprints were added). They arrive at Mapleton Stables, where they are greeted by the supervisor Silas Brown with a torrent of rude and abusive words. But Holmes whispers something in Silas Brown's ear, which immediately turns the bully into a submissive, trembling flunky. It turns out that Holmes tells Brown that he knows exactly what happened on the moor: how Brown found the horse and led him to his stable instead of to Colonel Ross's (the owner) stable.

How does Holmes know all this?

He has seen the horse's tracks in the moor going to its stable in King's Pyland, confirming the assumption that a horse normally returns to its stable. But then he noticed human tracks next to the horse's, now going in the direction of Mapleton Stables, which are run by the uncouth and aggressive Silas Brown. Holmes deduces that the man leading the horse to the competitor's stables must be Silas Brown. When confronted with this revelation, Brown at once changes his tune.

But here Dr. Watson protests, with justification, "But his stables had been searched."

To which Holmes replies dismissively, "Oh, an old horse-fakir like him has many a dodge." Admittedly, this is not a very convincing argument.

The (yet unspecified) suspicions against Straker the trainer intensify. Holmes replies to a question by Inspector Gregory about the curious incident of the dog in the nighttime,

> *"The dog did nothing in the nighttime. That was the curious incident.*

The dog did not bark on the night of the crime. It did not bark because the trainer was familiar to him. However, this is a weak argument, as the dog did not bark at Simpson, a complete stranger acting in a noisy and eccentric manner.

And yet, Straker was the only one with access to the stable boy's dinner, a dinner consisting of a curried dish that was spiked with powdered opium. Still, what could be the trainer's motive?

Holmes predicted that a dejected Silas Brown would bring Silver Blaze to the race by disguising him. All that was needed was a rag dipped in spirits of wine to remove the paint from the horse's brow and legs and restore those distinctive white markings that had earned him the nickname "Silver Blaze."

Then, to everybody's astonishment, Holmes points to the horse as the perpetrator of the trainer's murder. It transpires that the frightened horse kicked its trainer in the forehead when the latter tried to maim him.

Holmes now details the chain of events and explains what led him to his conclusions.

As soon as Holmes realized that the key to solving the case is the doctored dish served to the stable boy, Hunter, while the horse was taken away, he concluded that Simpson had no access to the food; only the trainer had. And in this case, the dog that did not bark in the nighttime comes in: the dog knew the trainer and therefore did not bark.

This is not a very persuasive argument considering that the dog did not bark at Simpson either when the latter came to the stable, even though Simpson was a total stranger.

Thus, it was the trainer who came to the stable in the dead of night and took the horse away. But what was his purpose? Surely a nefarious one! The key is in the objects found in the trainer's pockets: a delicate surgical knife with which to cut a tendon in the horse's leg, to render him lame so he would not win tomorrow's race. Meanwhile, the trainer has put his bet on a rival horse, while most people have put their money on the favorite.

However, here Holmes's argument is rather weak: why did the trainer have to take the horse out of the stable? The stable boy, Hunter, was in a stupor, having been drugged, and the dog knew him well so it did not bark. So, why take the horse out of the stable? Moreover, it was impossible to perform such a delicate operation on a horse in pitch darkness. There was a lantern in the stable, which the trainer could use to carry out his evil plot.

The receipt for a high sum of money paid for a woman's dress that was found in the trainer's pocket indicates that he was dishonest in his domestic affairs, as well as in his professional life.

Holmes's surmise that the trainer could perform a delicate operation on the horse by the light of a candle in the middle of the moor is not very convincing. Moreover, the fact that Simpson's cravat was found in the dead trainer's hand is also not satisfactorily explained.

The problem resides not with Sherlock Holmes but with the author, Arthur Conan Doyle, who would not let a dog bark at a total stranger; who has the trainer taking the horse out of the stable into a dark moor; it would have been much easier to maim the horse's tendon inside the lighted stable, since the stable boy was already drugged with opium. The horse was abducted by its trainer, who took it to a dark and soggy moor.

When the trainer tried to harm the animal's leg, the frightened horse kicked him in the forehead with his steel shoe, causing him to drop to the ground and die. Thus, taking the horse out on the dark and gloomy moor in order to do it mischief proves to be a rather illogical move. And so is the fact that the dog did not bark.

But in contrast to these two rather dubious propositions, Holmes exhibits shrewdness and competence when he insists that only solving the mystery of the horse's disappearance will lead to solving the mystery of the murdered trainer.

THE MASTER OF MYSTERY
THE STORY *THE MAN WITH THE TWISTED LIP*

The story opens with a foreshadowing exposition, which centers round the addiction to opium, and the havoc that the substance has wreaked on the body of Isa Whitney, a friend of Dr. Watson's. Whitney's hysterical wife bursts into the house of Watson and his wife late one night and franticly tells them that her husband has not come home in two days.

Dr. Watson volunteers to look for his missing friend in an opium den and to bring him home. This is the proleptic motif of the exposition: an addiction (to opium). However, at the center of the story, is an addiction to panhandling which, in fact, turns out to be very lucrative.

In the first paragraph we are given a description of the opium addict, the slave to the drug, "...*yellow, pasty face, drooping lids, and pin-point pupils... a wreck and a ruin.*"

This foreshadows the description of the beggar who comes later in the story:

> *A shock of orange hair, a pale face disfigured by a horrible scar which, by its construction, has turned up the outer edge of his upper lip, a bulldog chin, and a pair of very penetrating dark eyes which present a singular contrast to the color of his hair...*

Here we have a foreshadowing clue, suggesting that this is merely a disguise, a facade, since in real life, a "shock of orange hair" hardly ever goes with "penetrating dark eyes."

Another clue in the exposition points to a pretense, an affectation found in the description of Holmes in the opium den:

> *... a tall, thin, old man, with his jaw resting upon his two fists, and his elbows upon his knees, staring into the fire.*

Another foreshadowing clue pointing to Isa Whitney's opium addiction is the fact that when he was in college, he read De Quincy's description of his dreams, and soon afterwards, he began to indulge in the habit. Similarly, the main protagonist of the story, the beggar, acquired in drama school the skill of disguise and make-up and consequently, became a professional beggar, a habit he could not kick because of the enormous gains it brought him.

Thus, the foreshadowing exposition creates anticipatory analogies in the story, predicting developments and events, and even the final conclusion, since masks and disguises are bound to be removed eventually, which is what happens to our protagonist, Neville St. Clair.

At the beginning of the story, when Dr. Watson is at the opium den, we are told:

> *The bedroom window was a broad one and opened from below. On examination traces of*

blood were to be seen upon the window-sill, and
several scattered drops were visible upon the
wooden floor of the bedroom.

Mrs. St. Claire later tells Sherlock Holmes, "On the very day that I saw him last, he cut himself in the bedroom." Here we have a direct link between the husband and the beggar. It is clear that they are one and the same person, as both bleed profusely from a cut that took place in a bedroom.

In this way, the wife's claim that she saw her husband in the window of the house by the wharf is substantiated. And the assertion that the husband was alive and unhurt is also confirmed: the blood was from a slight cut he had suffered earlier. In other words, nobody forced the husband to be in that room above the opium den; it was his own choice to occupy that dingy place. If nobody forced him to be there, why then was he there?

This will be revealed only at the end of the story.

In both the foreshadowing exposition and the main story, the wives are described as a frightened, nervous women. Isa Whitney's wife is described as:

... suddenly losing her self-control. She ran
forward, threw her arms around my wife's neck
and sobbed upon her shoulder.

Whereas Neville St. Clair's wife

... stood with her figure outlined against the
flood of light, one hand upon the door, one half

raised in her eagerness... with eager eyes and
parted lips, a standing question.

There is an analogy between the husband and the beggar in the way they are described standing by the window:

There were, it is true, some blood stains upon his
right shirt-sleeve, but he pointed to his ring
finger, which had been cut near the nail, and
explained that the bleeding came from there,
adding that he had been to the window not long
before, and that the stains which had been
observed there came doubtless from the same
source.”

Mrs. St. Clair had seen her husband standing by the window, we were told earlier:

The window was open, and she distinctly saw
his face.

These are the facts we know so far: the husband cut his hand and it bled; the beggar cut his hand and it bled. Both accidents happened on the same day and in a bedroom.

The husband stood by the window “*...beckoning to her from a second floor window.*”

The beggar states that “*... he had been to the window not long before...*”

About the husband we are told that “*he wore some dark coat,*” and about the beggar we are told that he had “*...penetrating dark eyes which present a singular contrast* *to the color of his hair...*" hinting that it is a disguise. Isa Whitney became addicted to opium as a result of his college experiences; the husband became addicted to lucrative panhandling and does so with the help of tricks of the trade that he learned in drama school.

When we first come across Isa Whitney he is described thus:

> *Yellow, pasty face, drooping lids and pin-point pupils, all huddled in a chair, the wreck and ruin of a noble man.*

And the beggar is described thus:

> "*A shock of orange hair, a pale face, disfigured by a horrible scar, which by its contraction, has turned up the other edge of his upper lip, a bulldog chin and a pair of very penetrating dark eyes...*"

The beggar is referred to as "a cripple," whereas Dr. Watson's friend, the opium addict, is described as "the wreck and ruin of a noble man." Thus, just as behind the addict is found a decent, upstanding man, behind the beggar, too, is found a decent upstanding man.

Sherlock Holmes himself hides behind a façade, masquerading as a regular drug addict in the opium den:

> *... a tall, thin, old man, with his jaw resting upon his two fists and his elbows upon his knees, staring into the fire.*

And later:

> *"...very wrinkled, bent with age, an opium pipe dangling down from between his knees, as though it had dropped in sheer lassitude from his fingers."*

Here we are given another reference to the theme of masquerade and disguise that is at the heart of the story.

Another foreshadowing hint pointing to the phony beggar comes when St. Clair's overcoat is found, its pockets stuffed with pennies and halfpennies collected by the beggar. One wonders what prompted the beggar to get rid of the coat, while the rest of St. Clair's clothes were found in the beggar's room? And why would the beggar try to dump the coat in the river (by stuffing the pocket with metal coins)? Surely, that does not help prove his innocence. Since there is no apparent advantage to the beggar in throwing the coat in the river, it is clear that the beggar is innocent and that it was someone else who got rid of the coat. But why? Judging by all the foreshadowing clues, only Neville, disguised as a beggar, could have done it.

Holmes makes one mistake, though. When Mrs. St. Clair asks, "You think he is dead?" Holmes says, "I do." The reason for this mistake is presumably to give Sherlock Holmes some "human flaw."

The word "dark" appears only twice in the story. The beggar's eyes are described as "dark and penetrating." They stand out in the beggar's appearance. Neville's coat is described a couple of times as dark. There is a "literary" link between the two, and with the help of the other foreshadowing clues, we can deduce that the beggar and Neville are one and the same person.

In order to solve the mystery early—even earlier than Sherlock Holmes does—one needs to note the following things:

* The word 'dark' is mentioned only twice through-out the story, in connection with the lost man (dark coat), and in connection with the beggar (dark penetrating eyes).

* The fact that the dark penetrating eyes of the beggar stand in contrast to the color of his hair and to his general appearance indicates that his revolting face is nothing but a mask (reminiscent of the scene in the opium den where Holmes himself pretended to be a shriveled old man in a trance.)

* Both the beggar and the lost man had their hand injured on the same day and both bled from the finger. And in both cases it happened in a bedroom.

* Both the 'lost' man and the beggar stand by the window of the room above the opium den.

* The opium addict's repulsive appearance, we are told, hides someone who was once a "noble man," suggesting that the beggar's repulsive appearance also hides a decent man.

* All these clues point to the fact that Neville and the beggar are one and the same.

* In fact, the reader can solve the mystery of the beggar/lost man even before Sherlock Holmes himself reaches his conclusions.

At the end of the story Holmes refuses to divulge the deductions that led him to the solution,

> *"I reached this one," said my friend, "by sitting upon five pillows and consuming an ounce or shag."*

This is not a proper answer to Dr. Watson's question, or to the reader who has not yet figured out the solution. But the intricate network of analogies between the foreshadowing exposition and the rest of the story makes for a complex, meticulously constructed, and sophisticated story.

WHO NEVER SHOWED UP
AT CHURCH?
THE STORY *A CASE OF IDENTITY*

*'You have heard about me, Mr. Holmes?' she
cried, 'Else how could you know all of that?'*
*'Never mind,' said Holmes, laughing, 'It is my
business to know things. Perhaps I have trained
myself to see what others overlook.'*

Like many Sherlock Holmes stories, this one, too, opens
with Holmes and Dr. Watson sitting by the fire discussing
topics that have to do with crimes of various sorts.
Holmes claims that the bigger the crime, the simpler it is
to solve, while the smaller ones are more intriguing and
challenging. The story immediately supplies two metaphors that support this claim:

*He [Sherlock Holmes] held out his snuffbox of old
gold, with a great amethyst in the center of the
lid. Its splendor was in such contrast to the
homely ways and simple life that I could not help
commenting upon it.*

Holmes explains that the snuffbox is a gift from the King of
Bohemia in return for assistance in solving a case that lay
heavily on the king's soul. An equally splendid ring that

sparkled on Holmes's finger turned out to be a souvenir from the reigning family of Holland. The golden snuffbox with the precious stone in its center, like the brilliant ring, so incongruous with the simple, uninspired life that Holmes leads, are concrete metaphors illustrating his argument that it is the seemingly trivial, banal, and simple cases that turn out to be the most interesting and challenging.

This is how Holmes describes his method of solving crimes:

> *A certain selection and discretion must be used in producing a realistic effect... This is wanting in the police report, where more stress is laid perhaps upon the platitudes of the magistrate than upon the details, which to an observer contain the vital essence of the whole matter.*

A visibly upset young woman shows up on Holmes's doorstep and, in great agitation, tells him and Dr. Watson that her fiancé disappeared just before the wedding. She has not heard from him since. She met the man, Mr. Hosmer Angel, at a get-together organized by her church. There was something eccentric and peculiar about him, but she never gave it a second thought. For example, he insisted on typing all his letters to her on a typewriter, never writing any of them by hand—a hint that he is trying to hide his true identity, which may be recognized by someone who knows him. Moreover, the young woman says, *"He would rather walk with me in the evening than in the daylight, for he said that he hated to be conspicuous."*

This is another sure indication that he is trying to conceal his true identity. And then she adds:

> *Very retiring and gentlemanly he was. Even his voice was gentle... as result of some childhood illness, ... it had left him with a weak throat and a hesitating, whispering fashion of speech.*

Hosmer Angel obviously disguises his voice so that his young fiancée—who presumably knows his real voice well—won't recognize him.

Thus, even at this early stage of the unfolding of the plot, it is quite clear to the reader that the eccentric fiancé is not who he appears to be, and that he is trying hard to camouflage his true identity from his young fiancée.

Later in the story, the young woman shows Holmes a missing person ad that she has published in the papers in an attempt to locate her missing fiancé. In it she gives the following description:

> *About five feet seven inches in height; strongly built, sallow complexion, black hair, [...] bushy black side-whiskers and mustache; tinted glasses; slight infirmity of speech...*

This is an apt description of someone trying hard to disguise his identity from a person who knows him well. The only man whom the young fiancée, Mary Sutherland, knows well is her stepfather, Mr. Windibank.

There are other clues throughout the plot indicating that the missing fiancé tried to conceal his true identity.

He never gave the young woman his address. She was to mail all her letters to this address: the Leadenhall Street Post Office, not to the company where he worked, which he did not disclose.

In the ad that was put in the papers, the mysterious fiancé is described as "*five feet seven inches in height... strong build...*," a description that also fits James Windibank, the stepfather, who is described as follows: "*The man [the stepfather] was a sturdy, middle-sized fellow.*"

We learn that the stepfather and the fiancé have never met! Whenever the fiancé came to the young woman's house, the stepfather was reported to have gone on a business trip to France. But in fact, he stayed in London and disguised himself as the fiancé.

The young woman tells Holmes and Watson:

> *I wrote to Father at Bordeaux, where the company has its French offices, but the letter came back to me on the very morning of the wedding.*

This clearly suggests that the stepfather was in town pretending to be the fiancé.

Thus, before Sherlock Holmes presents his solution to the mystery, the reader already possesses several indicators that it is the stepfather who is presenting himself as the fiancé. The only question remaining is the motive. Why did he do it? The answer is simple: for money. A short time after her husband's death, Mary's mother married a man fifteen years her junior. Upon her husband's death, the widow inherited a thriving business. The stepfather prevails on his wife to sell the business for the hefty sum of 4,700 pounds sterling. In addition, he took control of his stepdaughter's annual income of 100 pounds bequeathed to her by an uncle. The young woman assures Holmes that she could easily subsist on half that sum.

Clearly, when the young woman gets married and lives in her own house, the stepfather stands to lose the hefty sum he draws each quarter from her account. Understandably, he would do whatever he can to thwart her chance to get a husband.

She explains to Holmes:

> He [Mr. Windibank, the stepfather] never did
> wish us to go anywhere. He would get quite mad
> if I wanted so much as to join a Sunday School
> treat. ... and he said that I had nothing to wear...

The stepfather insisted that a young woman should be content to stay with her immediate family:

> "Well, you know, Father didn't like anything of
> the sort. He wouldn't have any visitors if he
> could help it, and he used to say that a woman
> should be happy in her own family circle."

The young woman, however, refuses to be confined to her family circle; she is eager to meet a young man and get married. In order to foil her matrimonial plans, the stepfather disguises himself as a young suitor, thus making sure that no wedding would take place.

All this information and the conclusions derived from it are presented to the reader at various stages of the plot, and long before Holmes details his own solution to the mystery.

The stepfather realizes that he cannot sustain the subterfuge indefinitely. His only solution, then, is to make the fiancé disappear from his stepdaughter's life, breaking her heart in such a way that she will not attempt to find another young man in the foreseeable future.

The stepfather wastes no time in carrying out his new scheme:

> *"Mr. Hosmer Angel came to the house again, and proposed that we should marry before Father came back. He was in dreadful earnest, and made me swear, with my hands on the Testament, that whatever happened, I would always be true to him."*

Thus, the scheming stepfather paves the way for his retreat; he prepares his stepdaughter for his disappearance, ensuring that heartache and distress will prevent her from ever contemplating matrimony again.

At the denouement Sherlock Holmes takes the required steps: he recapitulates in detail the whole mystery, tracing its development; he points out the motivation and the reasons for the actions taken, and then lays out his solution.

A young man in his early thirties marries a widow fifteen years his senior so he can inherit her substantial possessions. He then gains control of her young daughter's income. Fearing that the young lady (who is in her early twenties) will find a husband and leave the house, depriving him of her yearly allowance, he uses any possible argument to dissuade her from seeking the company of her contemporaries. When he realizes that keeping her from going to social occasions and seeking a future husband is not feasible, he embarks on a course that, he believes, will separate her from the company of potential husbands.

Concealing his true identity, he disguises himself as a young man, and woos the young woman gently but resolutely, ending up winning her heart. The stepfather knows full well that he cannot keep up this charade indefinitely, so he brings matters to a head by proposing and then disappearing at the threshold of the church where they were to be married. The young woman is left grieving and brokenhearted, despairing of ever finding another husband. Thus, the scheming stepfather secures his control of the young woman's income.

Those are the facts, and they are already known to the perceptive reader who can identify and interpret the many clues strewn along the text, easily reaching the right conclusion, long before Holmes's exposition. We have here a clever, sophisticated union of three components: a clever author, a clever detective, and a clever reader.

THE CASE OF THE MARRIED BACHELOR
THE STORY
THE ADVENTURE OF THE NOBLE BACHELOR

This is the story of Lord Robert St. Simon, who got engaged and then married a charming, attractive young girl named Hatty Doran, the daughter of a California millionaire who made his money mining gold. A short while after the wedding ceremony in the church, as Lord St. Simon's family sat down to a festive breakfast, the bride got up, muttered some words of apology, and retired to her room. She was never seen again. Lord St. Simon, haughty and supercilious, comes to seek professional advice from Sherlock Holmes in an attempt to locate the missing bride.

Before the nobleman shows up at Holmes and Watson's residence, Holmes makes the following comment about the "fashionable epistle" that came in the morning mail:

> *Yes, my correspondence has certainly the charm*
> *of variety ... and the humbler are usually the*
> *more interesting.*

However, the case of the heartbroken bachelor, scion to one of the most elevated families of the realm, intrigues Holmes and piques his curiosity. He admits that the case holds more interest for him than he has initially thought:

They often vanish before the ceremony, and
occasionally during the honeymoon, but I cannot
call to mind anything quite so prompt as this.

The missing bride's father and her new husband, the Lord, turn to the police for help. Here we have an extra-textual generic convention that presumably originated with Don Quixote and Sancho Panza: pitted against the clever, insightful, methodical detective (Sherlock Holmes) is a police investigator (Inspector Lestrade, in this case) who is a bumbling fool, lacking in imagination and inspiration. The incompetence of the police is made apparent very early in the unfolding of the plot. An embarrassing incident takes place right after the wedding ceremony:

It appears that some little trouble was caused by
a woman [Flora Millar]... who endeavored to
force her way into the house after the bridal
party, alleging that she had claim upon Lord St.
Simon. It was only after a painful and prolonged
scene that she was rejected by the butler and
the footman.

The police lose no time reacting:

That Miss Flora Millar, the lady who had caused
the disturbance, has actually been arrested.

On the one hand, we have here the typical generic convention that shows the police acting foolishly and erroneously, being incapable of separating the wheat from the chaff, but on the other hand, perhaps in this case it is not so, since Flora Millar's disrupting the wedding party, claiming to have had a long intimate affair with the Lord, actually suggests that she may have colluded in the disappearance of the bride. However, the Flora Millar incident becomes even more convoluted and enigmatic. The missing bride, it turns out, was seen later walking with *"this very woman"* i.e., Flora Millar. Could Flora have a part in the bride's disappearance after all? But then we learn that the bride showed no sign of being inconvenienced or threated by Flora Millar.

The pendulum swings from suspicion to vindication: Flora Millar is first implicated, then absolved. Lord St. Simon explains to Holmes:

> *That is what Mr. Lestrade, of Scotland Yards, looks upon as so serious. It is thought that Flora decoyed my wife out and laid some terrible trap for her.*

The fact that this is the police's assumption—which is bound by convention to be spurious and erroneous—takes Flora Millar off the hook. But the pendulum swings back when Lord St. Simon tells Holmes, *"I do not think Flora would hurt a fly."*

Here Holmes himself pushes the pendulum in the other direction, throwing more suspicion on Flora Millar by saying, *"Still, jealousy is a strange transformer of character."* Adding soon afterwards, *"Circumstantial evidence is occasionally very convincing."*

The next scene, however, soon proves that focusing on Flora Millar and oscillating between suspecting her and clearing her are nothing but a clever ploy, a red herring, to deceive the reader and divert his/her attention from the main business. There is a turning point in the plot that almost stops the pendulum swing when it comes to Flora Millar's role. Inspector Lestrade finds a bundle of the missing bride's wedding clothes with a note in a pocket that says, *"You will see me when all is ready. Come at once."* The note is signed F. H. M.

Inspector Lestrade sees this as the ultimate proof of Flora Millar's culpability. Flora Millar, he says triumphantly, was responsible for the bride's disappearance. After all, her initials are on the note. But the time-honored convention of the detective genre assures us that the police are always on the wrong track.

When the lord departs, telling Holmes, *"Should you be fortunate enough to solve this problem...,"* the detective rejoins, *"I have solved it."*

But Holmes is not yet ready to share with the reader how he reached his dramatic conclusion. This lack of information urges the reader to explore another avenue of investigation, which up to now has been bypassed and neglected because of the Flora Millar hypothesis.

When the lord describes the unhappy turn of events at the church, he mentions that his wife's mood, which had been very upbeat before the church ceremony, became visibly sour and gloomy immediately afterwards:

> *"I saw then the first signs that I had ever seen*
> *that her temper was just a little sharp. The*

incident, however, was too trivial to relate and
can have no possible bearing upon the case.

But Sherlock Holmes, who knows only too well that it is precisely the little things that are truly important, and that the lord's perception is far from being reliable, urges his client to tell him the details of that seemingly unimportant incident that occurred near the altar:

> *Oh, it is childish. She dropped her bouquet as we*
> *went towards the vestry. She was passing the*
> *front pew at the time, and it fell over into the*
> *pew. There was a moment's delay, but the*
> *gentleman in the pew handed it up to her again,*
> *and it did not appear to be the worst for the fall.*
> *Yet, when I spoke to her of the matter, she*
> *answered me abruptly, and in the carriage, on*
> *our way home, she seemed absurdly agitated*
> *over this trifling cause."*

Indeed, one wonders why such a trivial incident would bring about such a drastic and dramatic change in the bride's spirits. It seems that herein lies the clue to solving the mystery. Holmes immediately pursues this line of inquiry:

> *'Indeed! You say that there was a gentleman in*
> *the pew. Some of the general public were present*
> *then?'... '*

'I call him a gentleman by courtesy, but he was quite a common-looking person. I hardly noticed his appearance.'"

Like the police inspector and, to some extent Dr. Watson, the lord's assumptions and observations are bound to be erroneous and unfounded. Indeed, Sherlock Holmes seems to be surrounded by nincompoops.

Since St. Simon dismisses the incident of the dropped bouquet, it must be obvious to the reader that this is a relevant and significant event. Since the dropping of the bouquet resulted in a dramatic change in the bride's mood, it is clear that the person in the pew—and not the fallen bouquet—is the cause of that change.

Who is that man, whose presence in the church during the wedding ceremony so affected the bride's spirit and demeanor? It is obvious that he is not English; the bride has arrived in England for the first time in her life and has spent her entire time since her arrival in the company of her father and her fiancé. She did not have any opportunity to meet an Englishman, let alone one who would elicit such a dramatic emotional reaction from her.

There is, therefore, only one conclusion: the man must be American. After all, the bride grew up in America, where undoubtedly she had ample opportunity to meet men. The haughty, condescending tone that Lord St. Simon employs when describing the man—insisting that the latter is no gentleman—is based on the fact that the man is not dressed as a typical English gentleman; therefore he must be an American.

The Case of the Married Bachelor

Seeing that the American has such tremendous emotional effect on the bride, prompting her to reject the matrimonial contract she has just entered, and in view of the servants' testimonies that there was no abduction but rather voluntary disappearance, it stands to reason that the man in the church incident is a former lover, perhaps even a husband.

Indeed, Holmes arrives at the very same conclusion. Since the note found in the bride's discarded clothes is a receipt from a hotel, it does not take Holmes long to track down the newly united lovers. He prevails on them to come to his apartment, where they meet the abandoned lord and tell him their story: how they met at a gold miners' camp in the West, fell in love, got married clandestinely, got separated, yet swore to be true to one another forever.

Presuming that her husband perished during an attack by Apache Indians, the young woman eventually consented to marry Lord St Simon. Her husband, however, having managed to escape from his Indian captors, tracks down his beloved, and finds her at the church by the altar. As in every respectable detective story, the plot is revealed when the mystery is solved. The extensive preoccupation with Flora Millar is further testimony to the sophistication of Sherlock Holmes fiction. This red herring—the alternative hypothesis that introduces suspicions and then discards them—eventually leads to another avenue of investigation. The swinging pendulum of incrimination and exoneration moves in a zigzag fashion, whereas the new investigation progresses in stages, each building on the previous one until the riddle is solved.

"I COME TO BURY CAESAR, NOT TO PRAISE HIM"
THE STORY *THE STOCKBROKER'S CLERK*

From the title of the chapter, one can deduce that it will focus less on Arthur Conan Doyle's literary excellence than on its failings, which are in evidence in the story *The Stockbroker's Clerk*. These flaws do not detract from the achievements of Conan Doyle's unique talent, which are still in evidence here, but they still need to be pointed out.

This is a story about a young stockbroker named Hall Pycroft who loses his position at a respectable stockbroking firm in the City. He has to compete with many other young brokers who are in the same predicament and are looking for jobs. His prospects are not good, and he has already used up his meager savings (70 pounds sterling). Luckily for him, he gets an offer from a great stockbroking firm on Lombard Street, offering him a more than adequate salary of 200 pounds.

A few days before Hall starts the new job, however, a strange man shows up on his doorstep. This brisk, energetic man, Mr. Arthur Pinner, extols and lauds Pycroft's financial ability and business acumen, which he claims he has heard from Pycroft's former employers. He presents himself as the owner of a vast business concern that has hundred of branches in France and England. The company's name is not mentioned, the visitor explains, because it does not wish the public to know about its extensive business. This assertive, aggressive man, whose tone of voice is forceful and frenzied, makes the young stockbroker an offer he can hardly refuse: Pycroft should resign from his new job and accept a position at the Franco-Midland Hardware Company which he, Pinner, runs with his brother. He offers him an astonishing annual salary of 500 pounds sterling, plus one percent commission on all the business done by his agents.

The young broker does have a few misgivings about the mysterious company and its somewhat eccentric owner, but the promise of such a generous offer plus a 100-pound note he is given as an advance, prevail on him to accept the unusual proposition. To his surprise, his new employer now presents a couple of conditions, *"mere formalities,"* as he says.

The first is that Pycroft state on paper that he is willing to act as business manager of the company for an annual salary of 500 pounds. Pycroft complies, and his new employer puts the paper in his pocket. This is unusual and contrary to accepted practice; it is the employer who should give the employee a letter offering him the job and detailing the conditions. But the young stockbroker is too dazzled by the new prospect, the high salary, and the 100-pound note to refuse.

The second condition is that Pycroft must not show up at work on Monday and not hand in his resignation. Mr. Pinner relates to him the altercation he had with the manager of the other firm regarding Pycroft, in which the former said, "*We picked him out of the gutter and he won't leave us so easily.*" The young broker is incensed at the insult and determines not to go to the office on Monday and not to hand in his resignation. The new employer is delighted and tells Pycroft he has to leave London, go to Birmingham, and report to Pinner's brother at the office there.

Several queries arise at this point: Why insist that the young broker not show up at the office of the company that has recently hired him? Why send him so promptly out of London? And why make him write a statement accepting the employment when it is the employer who should do so? Since the unconventional fellow insists on all these conditions, the question immediately arises: In what way does he stand to benefit from them?

There is a deviation here from the accepted employer-employee practice, and Mr. Pinner behaves bizarrely when he pockets the letter written by the new employee. It is obvious, then, that the new employer urgently needs a document written in the employee's handwriting, presumably in order to learn how to imitate the young broker's handwriting.

Since from the very beginning, the peculiar employer gives the impression that he is not on the level (even the young stockbroker senses it but he is too overwhelmed by the amazing salary and the 100-pound note), we can safely assume that copying the young broker's handwriting will serve some nefarious purpose later in the story.

Why does the new employer insist that the employee leave town right away? Why does he prevail on him not to go to the office where he was supposed to start working on Monday? The only possible conclusion is that an impostor is about to present himself in his stead, after having practiced imitating Hall Pycroft's handwriting.

The young stockbroker assures Sherlock Holmes that nobody at the Lombard Street firm has seen his face.

> '*I presume that nobody in the office had ever set eyes upon you,*" says Holmes.
> '*Not a soul,*' groaned Hall Pycroft.

Nor has his new employer seen his face, which raises the question: does it stand to reason that a respectable financial firm would hire a new employee without an interview, without ever setting eyes on him? This is a weakness in Conan Doyle's writing.

At the behest of his new and unconventional employer, Hall Pycroft leaves London and travels to Birmingham to meet Arthur Pinner's brother, who will confirm his employment at that extensive and august company.

To his utter astonishment, Pycroft can't even find the name of the firm on the door of the office. His suspicion that he has fallen victim to a nefarious scam increases. But then a man appears who looks very much like his London brother, except for his beard and hair color. When the two enter the building, Pycroft is struck by the shabby, dusty look of the office, which is furnished with just "*two deal chairs and a little table.*"

Suddenly the young broker realizes: there are not two brothers but only one person crudely disguising himself and impersonating the other. It is at this point that Hall Pycroft seeks the help of Sherlock Holmes. What is behind this charade? Why is one person faking the identity of another? We have already spotted one impostor who imitates the handwriting of the young broker. Here, then, is another impostor playing the part of "*two brothers,*" so he can remain in London and carry out some criminal activity and, at the same time, be in Birmingham attending to the young broker, burdening him with some absurd, Sisyphean tasks to ensure that he stays away from London and away from the firm where the impostor is impersonating him.

However, the text does not provide any information, not even a clue, about the connection between the two impostors and the dastardly deed that they are concocting. Conan Doyle here seems to be ignoring or challenging the basic tenet of the detective story, as formulated by Ellery Queen:

> *At this point in the story, you [i.e., the reader] are*
> *in possession of all the facts needed to build up*
> *a complete and logical solution of the crime.*"

In *The Stockbroker's Clerk*, only the last paragraphs of the story supply the information necessary for solving the mystery.

Hall Pycroft, Sherlock Holmes, and Dr. Watson pay a visit to "one of the brothers" in his dilapidated, grimy office. As soon as they walk in, they notice that the man is gripped by grief and horror:

> *His brow glistened with perspiration, his cheeks*
> *were of the dull, dead white of a fish's belly, and*
> *his eyes were wild and staring.*

A few minutes into the conversation, he excuses himself and goes to an adjacent room. When suspicious noises start emanating form that room, the three men break down the door and, to their great astonishment, discover that the man has hanged himself in the closet. They extricate him from the braces he tied around his neck, and under Dr. Watson's ministration, the man slowly revives and recovers. Now they turn their attention to the newspaper that Pinner had been reading, which supplies the explanation to what drove the man to such a desperate act.

It transpires that the man who attempted suicide and the impostor in the London office are indeed brothers. The newspaper account describes how the impostor waited for all the other employees to leave the building, then broke into the strong room and ransacked the safes, having first killed a watchman. The perpetrator was apprehended, and it turned out that he was the brother of a noted criminal. It is the latter who tried to commit suicide upon reading in the newspaper that the robbery in London had failed and that his brother was in custody.

But here Conan Doyle seems to have failed in maintaining a logical proportion between two actions. Is it credible that a hardened, notorious criminal would attempt suicide when he finds out (from a newspaper article) that his criminal sibling was arrested? The link between the two acts (the arrest of one brother and the suicide attempt of the other) is illogical and extreme, straining credulity. Here, too, we see the great master slipping. And this is in addition to concealing from the reader the motive that is behind the plot.

But for all its flaws, it is still an intriguing, appealing detective story worthy of Conan Doyle. Yet, because of the weaknesses I mentioned, "I come to bury Caesar, not to praise him."

MYSTERIES UNSOLVED
THE STORY *THE RESIDENT PATIENT*

The story opens with Sherlock Holmes and Dr. Watson returning from a nocturnal stroll in the streets of London, after a storm has subsided. They are surprised to find a young man (in his mid-thirties, by Watson's estimation) waiting in their apartment. He introduces himself as Dr. Percy Trevelyan, adding that he urgently needs Sherlock Holmes's professional advice.

There is a certain discrepancy between the young doctor's demeanor and what he says about himself. He appears to be meek and humble:

> *A pale, taper-faced man with sandy whiskers*
> *rose up from a chair by the fire as we entered.*
> *His age may not have been more than three or*
> *four and thirty, but his haggard expression and*
> *unhealthy hue told of a life, which has sapped*
> *his strength and robbed him of his youth. His*
> *manner was nervous and shy, like that of a*
> *sensitive gentleman, and the thin white hand,*
> *which he laid on the mantelpiece as he rose was*
> *that of an artist rather than of a surgeon.*

But here a surprise is in store for the reader, for despite his meekness and lifelessness, it turns out that the young man is quite proud of himself. He tells his listeners about his professional accomplishments:

*'I am a London University man... my student
career was considered by my professors to be a
very promising one. After I had graduated I
continued to devote myself to research ... and I
was fortunate enough to excite considerable
interest by my research into the pathology of
catalepsy, and finally to win the Bruce Pinkerton
prize and medal..."*

The discrepancy between the sad-sack appearance of the
young doctor and his self-confidence and conceit, is a clue
to other characters in the story whose exterior and out-
ward behavior camouflages hidden traits; what you see is
not what you get. The young doctor, despite his professional accomplishments, is struggling financially; his
impecuniousness prevents him from opening a clinic in a
respectable neighborhood of the city.

But one day an unexpected incident opened a new
prospect for him. A gentleman by the name of Blessington,
a total stranger to him, showed up in his room with a most
unusual offer. He was going to invest in the young doctor,
buying him a clinic in a fashionable neighborhood. The
visitor's demeanor was a bit brash and vulgar [compare
this to the *The Story of the Stockbroker*, where the protagonist was also approached by an eccentric, crude man who
made him an offer he could not refuse], but after slight
hesitation, the young doctor accepts the strange proposal.
After some negotiation they agreed on the conditions:

*I'll take the house, furnish it, pay the maids and
run the whole place. All you have to do is just*

*wear out your chair in the consulting room. I'll let
you have pocket money and everything. Then
you hand over to me three quarters of what you
earn and keep the other quarter for yourself.*

Blessington explains that he prefers investments to saving money in the bank, but his loud, vulgar behavior suggests that he has another, compelling secret motive. Thus, Blessington becomes the *"resident patient"* in the young doctor's house, claiming that he has a weak heart that needed constant medical supervision. This arrangement lasted a few years.

However, a few weeks prior to the young doctor's visit to Holmes's apartment, Blessington came to the doctor in a state of great agitation and spoke of a burglary committed in the West End. He determined to put stronger bolts on the doors and bars on the windows.

The young doctor tells Holmes and Watson:

*From his manner it struck me that he was in
mortal dread of something or somebody...*

Presumably, herein lies the secret motive for his behavior. Gripped by terrible fear for his life, Blessington wishes to be surrounded by people; a doctor's clinic, filled with patients most hours of the day, was a satisfactory arrangement for him.

The fear for his life also dictated his place of residence inside the house, next to the clinic on the ground floor, *"He turned the two best rooms on the first floor into a sitting room and a bedroom for himself."*

Blessington's anxiety and panic also explain his peculiar habits, "*He was a man of singular habits, shunning company and very seldom going out.*"

Late one night, two men show up at the clinic (having first sent a note announcing their intention to call). They are a very strange looking pair:

> *He was an elderly man, thin, demure and commonplace, [leaning on the arm of a] tall, young man, surprisingly handsome, with a dark, fierce face, and the limbs and chest of a Hercules.*

They present themselves as father and son, and it is the young man who does all the talking. He explains that his father is a Russian nobleman now residing in London. The father suffers from cataleptic attacks, the very sickness that is Dr. Trevelyan's area of expertise.

When the doctor suggests that the son remain in the room during the consultation, the young man reacts in an unexpected and peculiar manner:

> '*Not for the world,*' *he cried with a gesture of horror.* '*It is more painful to me than I can express. If I were to see my father in one of these dreadful seizures, I am convinced that I should never survive it. My own system is an exceptionally sensitive one.*'

This outburst and the young man's fearful reaction raise several questions: first, his claim that he won't be able to survive if he saw his father having a seizure defies logic. Second, the consultation can last at most an hour, whereas he stays with the old man day and night witnessing his seizures. Moreover, the tiny, frail old man and the Herculean, robust, young man hardly look as if they could be related. It is, therefore, clear that the young man, who purports to be so reluctant to stay with his father during the medical appointment, is eager (for a reason that becomes apparent only later) to remain by himself in the waiting room. It is obvious that the two men harbor some secret. This assumption gains corroboration from what happens next:

> 'Suddenly, however, as I sat writing, he [the old man] ceased to give any answer to all my inquiries, and on my turning toward him I was shocked to see that he was sitting bolt upright in his chair, staring at me with a perfectly bland and rigid face. He was again in the grip of his mysterious malady."

However, it soon becomes apparent that the episode has been nothing but a pretense, a subterfuge:

> 'I made a note of my patient's pulse and temperature, tested the rigidity of his muscles, and examined his reflexes. There was nothing markedly abnormal in any of these conditions, which harmonized with my former experiences.'

It is clear the old man is an impostor. But what does he stand to gain from such a deception? And why did the young man insist on staying in the waiting room during the examination? Did he try to get into other rooms in the house? If so, to what end? Why does the young man present the old man as his father? If the old man was trying to get the doctor out of the room, at least for a moment, how could he know that "nitrite of amyl," the medication the doctor was looking for, was not in the clinic, so the doctor had to go outside to look for it. Why did the old man want to leave the clinic, and why did he not leave with the young man?

Some of these queries lead to the following possibilities; the two men presenting themselves as father and son came to the clinic to look for something or someone. The old man pretended to be sick in order to focus the doctor's attention on him and allow the young man to explore the house at will.

Here is another flaw in the narrative. The doctor has already told Holmes and Watson that his eccentric employer, Blessington, lived in the rooms adjacent to the clinic and that he very rarely left the house. How, then, could the two impostors know that Blessington would be out of the house on that same day and at that same hour? Moreover, the following evening, the pair returns to the clinic, the old man engages the doctor in conversation while the young man, again, roams the house freely. The possibility that night after night they would come to the house of a man who hardly ever left the premises and never met the landlord who lives next to the clinic is illogical and strains credulity.

Shortly after the departure of the two, Blessington returns and is immediately seized with panic and rage. He has found several footprints on the carpet in his room (it is easy to deduce that they are the footprints of the gigantic young man). Blessington is so furious and distraught that he sits down and cries.

Here another error in the narrative can be detected. At the beginning of the story, we are told that Blessington's room is on the first floor; later on we are told that the doctor, Holmes, and Watson ascended to the room of the resident patient.

Some of the questions the text raises remain unanswered; some are unsolved even at the end. How could the old man and his young companion know that Blessington would not be home two nights in a row? Blessington is someone who leaves his home on very rare occasions, and then only for a very short time. Why did the two men leave the house stealthily and not openly, as they had come in? And then later, they come in announced again.

All these mysteries remain unsolved. The story seems to be ignoring the basic tenets of the genre of the detective story. An answer to the question—what was the purpose of the search in Blessington's room is found only in the last paragraphs, when we are told about the connection between the two men and Blessington. Thus, the reader has no way of answering these questions by himself/herself. The story violates the "fair chance" principle. Moreover, the inconsistency regarding the location of Blessington's room also contributes to the sense that this story is not well put together and was sloppily written.

At the young doctor's request, Sherlock Holmes and Dr. Watson pay a visit to the house. As they start to ascend the stairs, Blessington appears at the door shouting, "*I have a pistol... I give you my word that I'll fire if you come any nearer.*" When he recognizes the doctor and the other two gentlemen, he invites them to come up to his room. Watson is quite alarmed at the sight of the man:

> *He was fat, but had apparently at some time been much fatter, so that the skin hung about his face in loose pouches, like the cheeks of a bloodhound.*

Thus, while Blessington is described as a hunting dog, he is in fact the one hounded. When Holmes asks if he knows the people who are following him, he refuses to answer.

They go back home, only to be awakened early the next morning by an urgent message from the young doctor to come to his house at once. Upon arrival, they are told, "Blessington has committed suicide!" A police officer soon confirms that, indeed, Blessington has hanged himself.

It is the accepted convention in Sherlock Holmes stories that conclusions arrived at by police inspectors are always erroneous and wide of the mark. Indeed, Sherlock Holmes soon announces that Blessington did not commit suicide. "*It is a very deeply planned and cold-blooded murder.*"

The police inspector rejects Holmes's conclusion. "*Why should anyone murder a man in so clumsy a fashion as by hanging him?*" he asks, whereupon Holmes says, "*That is what we have to find out.*"

But no answer is forthcoming. Only at the very end is an explanation provided.

Holmes states confidently that three men were involved in Blessington's murder. Holmes is led to this conclusion by the four cigar butts found in the fireplace. Three are identical, one is different, which leads Holmes to conclude that the three belonged to the murderers and the fourth was smoked by Blessington. Similar Havana cigars were found in Blessington's pocket. Holmes states:

> *Having secured him [Blessington], it is evident to me that a consultation of some sort was held. Probably it was something in the nature of a judicial proceeding.*

There are two weaknesses in his conclusion. One, what was the purpose of the assassins' "consultation"? After all, they came to kill Blessington. They found him, possibly tied him with a rope, so what was there to discuss? After all, lingering at the crime scene can only lead to their exposure and arrest. Moreover, is it conceivable that the murderers would sit around and enjoy a leisurely smoke—and in the company of their victim!—prior to committing the crime?

Sherlock Holmes apparently does not detect these flaws in his argument. The fault is, in fact, the author's fault: it was he who planted the cigar butts in the ash tray. Only in the last couple of paragraphs does the author reveal the facts behind the case and solves the mystery.

It turns out that Blessington was a member of a crime ring, the Worthingdon Bank Gang," but he turned police informer, squealing on his partners and leading to the hanging of one member and the long incarceration of the other three. When they got out of prison, they vowed to avenge the death of their comrade and to kill the traitor.

Here, too, the author does not abide by the conventional principles of the detective story. He should have scattered clues along the text, allowing the intelligent and perceptive reader to solve the riddle before Sherlock Holmes spills all the beans and hands us the solution.

But for all its failings, it is still an intriguing, captivating story.

CRIME AND LATE PUNISHMENT
THE STORY *THE CROOKED MAN*

This is the story of Colonel Barclay and his wife Nancy. Barclay was the commander of an army regiment, a gallant veteran much respected and appreciated. His wife was known for her great beauty. In fact, several elements that appear at the beginning of the story provide useful clues for solving the mystery. The colonel, we are told, is greatly devoted to his wife, "*he was actually uneasy if he were absent from her for a day.*"

She, apparently, did not reciprocate the sentiment, "*She, on the other hand, ... was less obtrusively affectionate.*" And later the narrator reiterates, "*She was never... ostentatiously affectionate.*"

There is evidence that the uxorious colonel is inordinately attached to his wife and afraid to lose her:

> *Colonel Barclay himself seems to have had some singular traits in his character... there were occasions on which he seemed to show himself capable of considerable violence and vindictiveness. This side of his nature, however, appears never to have been turned toward his wife.*

When the couple later engages in a *"furious altercation,"* the wife berates and insults her husband (*"You coward!"*), the colonel remarks are

> *...subdued and abrupt, so that none of them were audible to the listeners. The lady's, on the other hand, were most bitter, and when she raised her voice, could be plainly heard.*

Thus, the picture we had earlier of a peaceful, loving marriage dissolves, due to various hints strewn along the text. We have a couple where the husband is afraid of losing his wife and a woman who does not love her husband. We are also told that guests were never invited to their house. These observations will play an important role in the process of unraveling the mystery.

We are told that besides the colonel's occasional bursts of violence and vindictiveness, there was also

> *... the singular sort of depression, which came upon him at times... For days on end, when the mood was on him, he has been sunk in the deepest gloom.*

Clearly, the colonel's extreme irascibility on the one hand, and his almost clinical depression on the other, suggest that he suffers from bipolar disorder.

To sum up, we have a husband who is fearful that his wife would leave him, a wife who does not love her husband, and a childless couple who never invites guests to their house. These facts paint a gloomy picture of conjugal life. One must bear in mind that in Victorian times, it was practically impossible for a woman to leave a marriage; the woman was, if not by legal definition, at least by custom and convention, property of her husband.

Colonel Barclay, we are told, has another, more extreme, character trait:

> *The latter peculiarity took the form of a dislike to being left alone, especially after dark. This puerile feature in a nature which was conspicuously manly had often given rise to comment and conjecture.*

A colonel, senior military commander, much decorated and appreciated, who has taken part in famous battles, is afraid to be left alone, especially in the dark? There can be only one reason: there is a person from his past, someone to whom he has done a terrible wrong, who haunts him, and he is afraid to be surprised by that person when he is alone in the dark. This clue, appearing at the beginning of the story, will prove to be a valid hypothesis when it comers to the night of the tragedy. On that night, Nancy, the colonel's wife, had gone with her friend and neighbor, Miss Morrison, to a charity event organized by their church. Mrs. Barclay seemed quite at peace when she left the house that night. But when she came back, she seemed to be in a very foul mood. The first incipient evidence for this is in the following passage:

> *Mrs. Barclay herself lit the lamp and then rang the bell, asking Jane Stewart, the housemaid, to*

*bring her a cup of tea, which was quite contrary
to her usual habit."*

When the maid arrived with the tea, she was surprised to
hear the colonel and his wife engaged in a heated bitter,
argument. In fact, the colonel's remarks were subdued and
abrupt and barely audible to the servants, whereas his
wife's voice was loud, acrimonious, and accusatory. "*You
coward!* " she reiterated. The name David was heard a
couple of time, and then the colonel's wife demanded:

*"What can be done now? Give me back my life. I
will never so much as breathe the same air with
you again! You coward! You coward!"*

At which point the colonel emits a dreadful cry, and the
woman responds with a piercing shriek. The coachman
rushes to the door and tries to force it open. But the door
is locked from the inside. He runs outside to the French
windows; this being summer, the windows are open, so the
coachman enters the room and finds his mistress
"*stretched insensible upon a couch*," whereas the colonel
sits in an armchair, "*stone dead in a pool of his own
blood.*"

The coachman tries to open the door from the inside,
but the key is not in the door, nor can it be found any-
where in the room. When the police arrive, they determine
that the cause of death is a violent blow from a blunt
weapon. Indeed, a club of carved hard wood is found on
the floor. But there is no blood on the club. The club was
part of a collection of weapons brought from the different

countries where the colonel had fought. Perhaps the colonel himself brought it into the room, considering his fear of being alone, especially at night.

Mrs. Barclay could not have killed her husband: no heavy blunt instrument was found nearby, and she herself was unconscious so that she could not have hidden it. Moreover, during the argument with her husband, she was standing (or sitting) facing him, whereas the wound was at the back of his head.

One important finding on the scene of the crime was the face of the colonel:

> *There was one thing in the case which had made the deepest impression upon all the servants and the police. This was the contortion of the Colonel's face. It had set,... into the most dreadful expression, of fear and horror, which a human countenance is capable of assuming. More than one person fainted at the mere sight of him, so terrible was the effect. It was quite certain that he had foreseen his fate, and that it had caused him the utmost horror.*

The reader already knows about the colonel's fear of being alone, especially in the dark. Who, then, did he see that night that caused his face to contort in such a frightening fashion? Sherlock Holmes has already drawn the conclusion: since the key was gone, and neither the colonel nor his wife could have taken it (he is dead in a pool of blood and she is unconscious) "... *therefore a third person must have entered the room.*"

But who is that person? Why would his presence cause the colonel such profound shock? Did that third person murder the colonel, or was the mere sight of him sufficient to frighten the colonel to such an extent that he fell off his armchair, hit his head on the fender so hard that the injury caused instant death. The colonel must have known all his life that someone from his past (presumably someone whom he had wronged) might show up one day and exert retribution. His contorted, horrified face testified that he had seen that man that evening (the third man in the room). This supports the assumption that the flabbergasted colonel fell down and smashed his head against the fender and thus died.

But we still don't know the identity of this mystery man, who is presumably connected to a dark chapter in the colonel's life. How and why did he show up at the colonel's house at a time when a bitter argument was taking place between husband and wife? What made the colonel's wife hurl such terrible accusations at her husband, while only a couple of hours earlier she had left the house calm and content? What happened to her during that time? Whom did she meet during her absence from the house? Did she run across that man who so shocked the colonel and brought about his demise? Did she know that man from way back? If so, what did he tell her that caused such an outburst of invective and hostility toward her husband? Could that other man have told her about the wrong he suffered at the hands of the colonel, and was it that which enraged and incensed her against her husband?

All these questions become conjectures that hopefully will soon turn into facts. But in the meantime, there is need for more information, so that the questions and conjectures can be turned into solid facts. This information is soon supplied, although in an incomplete manner.

The colonel's wife is the best witness to tell us what happened during the time she was away from the house. But she is lying in her bed unconscious. However, Holmes manages to obtain the following information: Mrs. Barclay was accompanied by a neighbor, a young woman named Miss Morrison. At first, Miss Morrison is reluctant to betray her friend's secret. But when Holmes tells her that Mrs. Barclay may be accused of murder, and that every piece of information may save her, Miss Morrison changes her mind. She tells him that on their way back from church, they encountered a man with a deformed body, crooked legs, and a drooping head:

> *"We were passing him when he raised his face to look at us in the circle of light thrown by the lamp, and as he did so he stopped and screamed out in a dreadful voice,*
>
> *'My God, it's Nancy!' Mrs. Barclay turned as white as death, and would have fallen down had the dreadful-looking creature not caught hold of her...she, to my surprise, spoke quite civilly to the fellow.*
>
> *'I thought you had been dead this thirty years, Henry,' said she, in a shaking voice.*
>
> *'So I have,' said he.*

'Just walk on a little way, dear,' said Mrs.
Barclay, 'I want to have a word with this man.
There is nothing to be afraid of'.
She tried to speak boldly, but she was still
deadly pale and could hardly get her words out
for the trembling of her lips."

The colonel's wife begged Miss Morrison not to tell anyone about what had happened, explaining only: "It is an old acquaintance of mine who has come down in the world."

The mystery is about to be solved. The third person in the room—who must have entered through the open door—is that same deformed wretch who accosted the two ladies. It is clear that he knows the colonel's wife from an earlier period in their lives. This is how the man is described as he is venting his fury at the colonel:

I saw the crippled wretch standing by the
lamppost and shaking his clenched fist in the air,
as if he was mad with rage.

His broken, misshapen body is presumably the result of the wrong that the colonel inflicted upon him in the past. He must have followed the colonel's wife to her home, instinctively, without knowing exactly what he was about to do. In the midst of the acrimonious argument between the colonel and his wife, he entered the room through the open door.

So far the conjectures sound logical and persuasive. We need one more piece of the puzzle to solve the case. What exactly happened in that room and how did the colonel die. Since the colonel is dead and his wife lies unconscious, only one man is left to provide that last piece of information and shed light on the story. This man is Henry Wood, the crooked man.

So Sherlock Holmes and Dr. Watson pay a visit to that miserable wretch in his rented room. And this is the story he tells them. Thirty years ago, Corporal Henry Wood was the best-looking soldier in the regiment. Barclay was a sergeant in the same unit, and both loved Nancy Devoy, daughter of the color-sergeant. Nancy was in love with Wood, but her father was set upon her marrying Barclay, who was better educated and held a higher rank. One day, the camp was surrounded by ten thousand rebels. A volunteer was needed to sneak around the rebel forces and contact another battalion to get relief.

Henry Wood volunteered for this perilous mission. Barclay was supposed to know the ground better than anyone in the camp, and he drew up a route around the rebel lines. Barclay was apparently aware of the fact that Nancy did not love him, and that she was, in fact, in love with the handsome corporal. This is not stated explicitly but it can be inferred from the fact that Barclay sent the brave and trusting Wood the wrong way, straight into a rebel ambush.

Later, hill dwellers murdered his captors and he became their slave for a time, until he managed to escape. Eventually he found himself among the Afghans who saved his life. After many years of physical and mental torture, his body became contorted and misshapen, his spirit irreparably broken.

Here Wood's story becomes a little vague. He tells Holmes and Watson that after thirty years absence, he longed to see the landscape of his native land once more. But he was determined not to see his beloved Nancy again because he did not want to present himself to her as crooked and deformed. Why, then, did he choose to live next to the army camp where her husband was the commander? He knew that Nancy had married the colonel. He must have been conflicted; he did not want his beloved to see him in such a wretched state, but yet he was curious and longed to see her. The latter sentiment must have prevailed (besides, she had already seen him in the street, so the shock had been somewhat blunted).

Wood's fury at the colonel, who had robbed him of his life, and the urge to take revenge on him, prompted Wood to follow Nancy home. He must have heard the quarrel between Nancy and her husband and the accusations of "coward" she hurled at him [and the twice mentioned "David", of which later].

Wood burst into the room in the middle of the fracas. As soon as the colonel saw him, his face contorted in unspeakable fright. Wood tells Holmes that he saw death in the colonel's face as soon as the latter laid eyes on him and recognized him. The colonel went over with his head on the fender:

> *But he was dead before he fell. I read death on his face as plain as I can read that text over the fire. The bare sight of me was like a bullet through his guilty heart.*

Crime and Late Punishment

The sophistication of *The Crooked Man* can be discerned from its beginning. There are clues dispersed along the text, and their cumulative effect gives rise to hypotheses and inferences that later acquire substantiation and confirmation.

In the colonel, we have a uxorious husband, whose wife does not requite his love—this clue later becomes confirmed when the two engage in an acrimonious argument, during which the wife hurls bitter accusations and insults at her husband, whereas his response is restrained and dejected. Another early clue is the fact that even when the colonel is having attacks of fury and violence, he never aims his wrath at his wife. Moreover, the fact that a decorated and esteemed soldier who was the commander in many battles is afraid to be alone in the dark can only have one logical explanation: in his military past, he must have done someone (a soldier? an officer?) a terrible wrong, and he is constantly afraid that that person might come to avenge that deed. This, indeed, comes to pass, and the ghastly expression on the colonel's face attests to the horror he must have experienced.

One question remains open: Who is that *David* the colonel's wife invokes when she so viciously castigates her husband? The colonel's name is James, and the name of her former lover, the victim of the colonel's evil machinations, is Henry. Since the *dramatis personae* of the story contain no male character by the name of David, we can assume that the wife refers to a historical or literary character. (At the beginning of the crooked man's confession, he mentions that the colonel was an educated man). The reference, then, is to another character that has committed an egregious wrong in order to obtain a woman (just as the colonel did in order to obtain Nancy).

That David, then, is the biblical King David who sent Uriah the Hittite to his death on the battlefield in order to get his wife Bathsheba. In the biblical story, God is mightily displeased with the king's behavior and He sends the prophet Nathan to tell the king the fable of the poor man and the ewe lamb. King David is reprimanded, but the wrong he had done is soon forgotten. Not so in the case of the colonel: his sin has not been forgotten and it comes back to haunt him and to end his life.

"SORRY, SIR, BUT YOU CAN DO BETTER"
THE STORY *THE RED-HEADED LEAGUE*

Sherlock Holmes and Dr. Watson receive a visitor: Mr. Jabez Wilson, owner of a pawnbroker business located not far from the City of London. Mr. Wilson appears a little shabby to Dr. Watson's eyes:

> *Our visitor bore every mark of being an average commonplace British tradesman, obese, pompous and slow... Altogether, look as I would, there was nothing remarkable about the man, save his blazing red head and the expression of extreme chagrin and discontent upon his features.*

In his little pawnbroker shop—which is almost empty of customers—Mr. Wilson employs an assistant named Vincent Spaulding. The latter is a model employee: smart, efficient, hard-working, meticulous, and on top of this, willing to work for half the customary wages. However, he seems to have one fault:

> *"Never was such a fellow for photography. Snapping away with a camera when he ought to be improving his mind, and then diving down*

into the cellar like a rabbit into its hole to develop
his pictures. That is his main fault.

The word "cellar" will recur only once more in the text, in connection with the cellar of a bank, which will be discussed later.

Mr. Wilson's assistant immediately piques the reader's interest, as well as the reader's suspicion. Why is he so industrious and so dedicated to the job that he is willing to work for half the wages? And what are those photos he is taking all the time? What is so special about the neighboring houses, that makes them worth photographing? How often can you shoot the same building? The assistant, then, arouses not just our interest but also our suspicion.

Next, the story focuses on a notice in the newspaper that Vincent Spaulding has brought to the attention of Mr. Wilson.

TO THE RED-HEADED LEAGUE
"On account of the bequest of the late Ezekiah
Hopkins, of Lebanon, Pa., U.S.A., there is now
another vacancy open which entitles members
of the League to a salary of four pounds a week
for purely nominal service. All red-headed men
who are sound in body and mind and above the
age of twenty-one years are eligible. Apply in
person on Monday, at eleven o'clock, to Duncan
Ross, at the offices of the League, 7 Pope's
Court, Fleet Street."

Sorry, Sir, But You Can Do Better

Vincent Spaulding, recently hired by Mr. Wilson, urges his boss, a man with flaming red hair, to submit his candidacy for this sinecure (garnering four pounds a week for minimal work). Mr. Wilson agrees to apply for the job.

He is told that the late American millionaire, Ezekiah Hopkins, who was also a red-head, bequeathed his fortune to a league of men, all having red hair.

Mr. Wilson tells Sherlock Holmes and Dr. Watson:

> *Vincent Spaulding seemed to know so much about it that I thought he might prove useful, so I just ordered him to put up the shutters for the day, and to come right away with me. He was very willing to have a holiday, so we shut the business up, and started off for the address that was given us in the advertisement.*

When they arrive at the appointed place, Mr. Wilson is stunned to see a multitude of red-headed men crowding the street. He feels discouraged and wants to head back, but Vincent Spaulding would not hear of it; he pushes and pulls, shoves and butts through the orange-tinted crowd until they reach the office.

Inside the small bare office is a short man, also with red hair, who introduces himself as Duncan Ross. After a short examination, Mr. Ross shakes Mr. Wilson's hand and announced that he is the lucky man chosen for the position. The work requires him to sit in the office every day for four hours (from ten in the morning until two in the afternoon) and diligently copy the *Encyclopedia Britan-*

nica. [Cf. a similar requirement in the story, *The Stockbroker's Clerk*].

Mr. Ross admonishes the newly hired employee. " You have to be in the office the whole time...If you leave, you forfeit your whole position forever." But Mr. Wilson, so pleased with a new job that offers lavish remuneration for minimal exertion, ignores the bizarre and suspicious conditions. What is this mysterious league of red-headed men? What is its purpose? How come the assistant, Vincent Spaulding, who is not red-headed, knows so much about it? And why did the assistant insist that his boss apply for the lucrative job? How did Spaulding manage to bring Mr. Wilson through the throng of red-headed applicants straight to the office? What is the meaning and purpose of the ridiculous Sisyphean work of copying the *Encyclopedia Britannica*? Why can't he leave the office even for a minute during the four hours of work? Is it not obvious that the absurd work and the prohibition to leave the office have only one purpose: to keep Mr. Wilson away from his shop for four hours every day?

In fact, Mr. Wilson does have a few doubts about the engagement:

> *... by the evening I was in low spirits again, for I had quite persuaded myself that the whole affair must be some great hoax or fraud, though what its object might be I could not imagine... Mr. Spaulding did what he could to cheer me up.*

Dr. Watson is right in his observation: the dedicated, resourceful assistant is up to his neck in the bizarre affair.

But despite the nagging doubts, Mr. Wilson cannot bring himself to pass up such a lucrative offer, especially since his pawnshop does not generate any income. Thus, he shows up at the Red-Headed League, where Mr. Duncan Ross awaits him and directs him to his desk where he is to start copying the first volume of the *Encyclopedia Britannica*. At first, Mr. Ross checks up on him periodically to make sure he does not leave the building, but after a while he trusts him and leaves him alone.

This routine continues uninterrupted for eight weeks, and at the end of each week, Mr. Wilson received his generous salary. And then suddenly, to his utter surprise, the whole business comes to an end. Upon arrival at the office, he finds the door locked and a note glued to it announcing, "THE RED-HEADED LEAGUE IS DIS-SOLVED. October, 9, 1890."

At this point, Mr. Wilson realized that the eight-week affair was nothing but a prank, but he is determined to get to the bottom of it, if only because he does not want to give up the substantial salary he was earning.

Sherlock Holmes is convinced that the assistant, Vincent Spaulding, is a key figure in this mystery, and he interrogates Mr. Wilson about his assistant. This is the information he receives. Spaulding had been in his employ a month before he called his attention to the advertisement. Spalding was one of a dozen applicants, and he was chosen *"because he was handy and would come cheap,"* for he was willing to work for half a salary. When asked what Spaulding looked like, Mr. Wilson replies:

"Small, stout-built, very quick in his ways, no hair on his face, though he's not short of thirty. Has a white splash of acid upon his forehead."

When Holmes hears this description, he immediately reacts:

Holmes sat up in his chair in considerable excitement. 'I thought as much,' said he, 'Have you ever observed that his ears are pierced for earrings?'

'Yes, sir, He told me that a gypsy had done it for him when he was a lad.'"

There is no doubt that Sherlock Holmes recognizes the criminal. In fact, some time afterwards, he says to Dr. Watson:

'Smart fellow that,' observed Holmes as we walked away. 'He is, in my judgment, the fourth smartest man in London, and for daring I am not sure that he has not a claim to be third. I have known something of him before."

So far, the information given to the reader is the following: Mr. Wilson's assistant, Vincent Spaulding, is in cahoots with the Red-Headed League; he contrived, and succeeded, in getting Mr. Wilson out of the pawnbroker's shop for four hours every day for eight weeks. We also know that he is a tireless photographer, taking pictures of the surrounding buildings, and then spending time in the cellar developing those pictures. There is no indication as to the purpose of those photos and what the assistant means to do with them. One suspects that he goes down to the cellar for a different reason. As mentioned earlier, the word 'cellar' appears only once more in the story, referring to a bank cellar. Since we already suspect that Vincent Spaulding may be a sneaky, cunning criminal, perhaps there is a connection between those two cellars, especially since one of them is in a bank.

Thus, the reader has several clues that may lead to a solution of the mystery. But from this point on, the story is somewhat disappointing. Dr. Watson asks Sherlock Holmes if he had gone to the pawnshop to see Vincent Spaulding. Holmes says, *"Not him."* *"What then?"* *"The knees of his trousers,"* is the dismissive, rather patronizing reply. Holmes obviously knows the answers to Watson's questions, but he disparages his faithful partner, leaving him to fumble in the dark. Next, Watson asks Holmes, *"Why did you beat the pavement* (with his stick)?" Again, Holmes answers condescendingly, *"My dear doctor, this is a time for observation, not for talk."*

Here the story challenges one of the distinctive ethical codes of the detective story genre: the detective must not conceal information from the reader. This infringement of the rules of fair play is even more blatant here because of the derisive, condescending rhetoric Holmes employs, especially when he stands at the corner of the street and declares:

> *"Let me see," said Holmes, sanding at the corner*
> *and glancing along the line, "I should like just to*

remember the orders of the houses here. It is a
hobby of mine to have an exact knowledge of
London. "

Holmes is not telling the truth. He is trying to memorize the layout of the street as part of his plan to prevent a crime that is about to be committed that night, a plan that is unknown to the reader.

Later that night, four people are gathered in Holmes's apartment on Baker Street: Holmes, Dr. Watson, Detective Jones of Scotland Yard, and Mr. Merryweather, a banker, who in spite of his name, looks sad-faced and gloomy. They leave the apartment and make their way to the cellar of the bank. The evocation of 'cellar' brings to mind the suspicious assistant Vincent Spaulding and his frequent visits to the cellar of Mr. Wilson's pawnshop, suggesting that Spaulding may be implicated in a crime against the bank.

Holmes, Watson, Inspector Jones, and the glum banker Merryweather hole up in the cellar, waiting for the crooks to carry out their heist. Sure enough, two robbers come out of a tunnel they have dug underneath the building. Holmes, Watson, and Jones overpower them (surprisingly easily, it must be said) and arrest them. The accomplice, it turns out, is the same red-headed man who had hired Mr. Wilson for the job at the Red-Headed League. The principal criminal is John Clay, aka Vincent Spaulding, "*murderer, thief, smasher, forger.*"

As often happens in Sherlock Holmes stories, the opening scene has the detective sitting with a new client, identifying (mostly by observing the latter's clothes and hands) the person's profession, traveling experience, mood, etc. The client is amazed at Holmes's ability to pick up so much personal information. Mr. Wilson, for example, has been to China, did some manual work, is a member of the Free Masons, and recently has done a lot of writing. This prologue is a kind of exposition that demonstrates to the reader Sherlock Holmes's amazing analytical and deductive abilities.

To some extent, the denouements of Sherlock Holmes's stories are analogous to their prologues. Here, too, Holmes sits with Dr. Watson and lays out in detail the solution to the mystery, explaining step by step how he cracked the puzzle and arrived at the conclusion.

In this story, it is Dr. Watson who listens (together with the reader) and admires the detective's keen analytical prowess. However, the conclusion exposes Holmes's weakness. Earlier, we noted Holmes's vague and insincere answers to Watson, which constituted a breach of the basic tenets of detective stories, i.e., the detective and the reader should be privy to the same reservoir of information. The fact that Holmes violates the ethical code of the detective story by evincing condescension and contempt underlines his failing and his error.

The main fault in the story is certainly the author's and not only Sherlock Holmes's. It has to do with the tunnel. Holmes states that as soon as he heard of the cellar in the bank, he realized that there was a connection to the cellar in Mr. Wilson's pawnshop, where the nefarious assistant would often go, purportedly to develop photographs of the run-down neighborhood. This is indeed a valid connection that an attentive, clever reader can discern. However, the idea that you can dig a tunnel in the heart of London, underneath a busy street from a cellar in a house to a cellar in a bank is quite preposterous. Bear in mind also Mr. Wilson's account that even before he began his sense-less work of copying the *Encyclopedia Britannica*, his assistant had already had a habit of descending to the cellar and spending time there. Thus, the crook could have easily continued to dig a tunnel while Mr. Wilson was on the premises. Why did he need to devise an elaborate ruse to drive Mr. Wilson out of the store? And why for only four hours a day? If getting rid of Mr. Wilson would make the job easier and more efficient, why not keep him out of the house for eight hours a day?

Moreover, we are told that Mr. Wilson was employed by the Red-Headed League for a period of eight weeks. Is it conceivable that a single person could dig an underground passage in the heart of London in such a short time? And what about water and sewage pipes? Surely, those would have complicated the work significantly. And what was done with the rubble amassed during the digging of the tunnel? How was it disposed of? True, the idea of excavat-ing a tunnel underneath the city is intriguing and exciting, but the logistics involved in such an undertaking surely makes it unrealistic if not absurd. And here is where the author errs, leading his protagonist to stumble and err with him.

And here is another weak point. We are told that while Holmes was pacing in the street in front of Mr. Wilson's store,

"Finally he returned to the pawnbroker's, and, having thumped vigorously upon the pavement with his stick two or three times, he went up to the door and knocked."

Later on, Sherlock Holmes explains to Dr. Watson that expecting a hollow sound, he was checking how deep the digging of the tunnel had gone and how far it was from the pawnbroker's shop. This, too, strains credulity, since it is inconceivable that a knock on the pavement with a cane would locate and detect an empty space the size of a tunnel.

This is another instance where the author, and Holmes with him, are found wanting. It is a pity. The plot of the story is intriguing and attractive, but the failures and lapses that strain credulity vitiate the story and detract from its realism.

"Sorry, sir, but you can do better."

WHEN MURKY SECRETS SURFACE
THE STORY *THE BOSCOMBE VALLEY MYSTERY*

The facts of the story are as follows: In the Boscombe Valley in Herefordshire, near the pleasant little town of Ross, lived two gentlemen from Australia, who had made their fortune in the gold mines there. One was John Turner who was very wealthy; the other was Charles McCarthy, a man of modest means. Turner allowed McCarthy to live rent-free (as becomes clear later) on part of his estate. Turner had an eighteen-year old daughter named Alice; McCarthy had a son, about the same age, named James. Turner and McCarthy appeared to have led rather retired lives, avoiding the society of their neighbors. Turner was known as a quiet, easygoing person, while McCarthy was hot tempered, irascible, and violent.

On Monday, the third of June, Charles McCarthy was seen leaving his home and making his way toward a little lake near Boscombe Valley. Two witnesses later testified that they had seen James, McCarthy's son, walking along the same way as his father (though the latter could not have seen him) with a gun under his arm. A short while later, another witness saw McCarthy and his son standing by Boscombe Pool, engaged in a loud and violent quarrel. McCarthy used very strong language to his son, and the latter was seen raising his hand as if to strike his father.

Next, the son was seen running to a nearby lodge, reporting that he had found his father dead in the wood at the edge of the lake. He was visibly excited, without either his gun or his hat, and his right hand and sleeve were stained with fresh blood. Soon afterwards, McCarthy was indeed found dead, stretched out on the grass beside the pool, having been hit on the head with a blunt instrument, which might have been the butt end of a gun. Here a question arises. If the son intended to murder his father, why did he not shoot him with a gun, instead of beating him on the head, which may have resulted in his losing consciousness, but not necessarily with his death.

But let us leave these questions and reservations aside, and return to the main facts. The young man was immediately arrested and accused of murdering his father. Some of his answers—or rather his refusal to answer—seemed to incriminate him. James McCarthy is warned by the investigator that his reticence makes him look more suspicious, but he remains adamant. When asked about the quarrel with his father, he refuses to supply any explanation. He admits, though, that the cry "*cooee*" was a signal that both he and his father had used in the past. Why then, did the father cry "*cooee*" even though he was not aware that his son was following behind him? Young James has no explanation for that.

James also testifies that when he rushed to his injured father, he seemed to have noticed a gray coat lying on the grass. But when he looked again later, the gray coat was gone. In reply to the investigator's question, he said that he had no idea how that happened. Sherlock Holmes, on the other hand, insists that the absence of clear answers in fact testifies to young James's innocence. James makes no attempt to invent answers that would exonerate him. He answers truthfully, even when his answers or lack of answers threaten to send him to the gallows.

Alice, Mr. Turner's young daughter, confirms that her father and McCarthy first met in Victoria, in the Australian gold mines. Curiously, Turner has become a very wealthy man, while McCarthy remained impecunious, depending on Turner's munificence to the extent that he lives rent-free on Turner's property. This is particularly intriguing in view of the fact that McCarthy has an irascible, violent temperament and people tended to avoid him.

James McCarthy is in love with Alice, but he refrains from proposing to her because of some unsavory secret in his past. When he was very young and reckless, he married a barmaid in town. Being trapped in that adolescent commitment, he cannot marry Alice. His father, on the other hand, is furious at his son's refusal to marry Alice and insists that he do so, using threats and violence. Turner is vehemently opposed to the union of James and Alice.

At this point, readers have at their disposal almost all the information needed for solving the mystery. A question arises: if Turner and McCarthy are so close that Turner allows McCarthy to live on his estate for free, why is he so vehemently opposed to McCarthy's wish that his son James marry Alice? Bearing in mind that McCarthy is a repulsive person, what accounts for the generosity shown him by Turner?

One is bound to wonder about the relationship between the two Australians. Two possibilities exist: one is that, despite McCarthy's problematic personality, Turner has a liking for him. The second may be the fact that Turner, who left the Australian gold mines with great wealth, is being continuously blackmailed by McCarthy. The last straw, from Turner's point of view, must be McCarthy's latest demand, that he allow his only daughter Alice to marry James. Turner understands full well what lies behind this proposal: a union between the two would make it easy for McCarthy to take over Turner's property and wealth. Turner must have come to the end of his tether, deciding that the last demand was totally unacceptable to him.

The reader must wonder: does McCarthy possess some secret knowledge about Turner, some damning piece of information that harks back to their common past in Australia? Does this knowledge give McCarthy power over Turner and allows him to blackmail him? This seems a valid conclusion, which lets various details and elements of the plot to fall into place.

Having made a fortune in the gold mines, Turner immigrated to England, becoming a wealthy landowner. McCarthy, on the other hand, remained poor. Somehow he managed to locate Turner in England and began to extort him.

We heard earlier that the signal word "*cooee*" was habitually used by McCarthy and James. We also noted that James could not explain why his father used the signal even though (as James insists) he had no way of knowing that James was following him.

Now this becomes clear, as Sherlock Holmes explains:

The 'cooee' was meant to attract the attention of whoever it was that he had the appointment with. But 'cooee' is a distinctly Australian cry, and one which is used between Australians. There is a strong presumption that the person whom McCarthy expected to meet at Boscombe Pool was someone who had been in Australia.

Thus, the veil of mystery has been removed, exposing the solution. McCarthy knew only one other Australian, Turner. They both arranged to meet. McCarthy was going to once more put the squeeze on Turner, to force him to agree to the marriage of James and Alice, and Turner wanted to put an end to this last extortion. Turner had only one option: to put an end to the life of the blackmailer.

Thus, Turner had a very strong motive, and he had the opportunity; they were alone at the edge of the wood by a remote lake. He also had the physical ability to carry it out, as transpired from Holmes's examination of the tracks by the lake.

All these arguments (even the circumstantial evidence) receive their validation in the last scene, when Turner meets with Sherlock Holmes and Dr. Watson. Turner's physical capability is evident despite his illness:

The man who entered was a strange and impressive figure. His slow, limping step and bowed shoulders gave the appearance of decrepitude, and his hard, deep-lined craggy features, and his enormous limbs showed that he was possessed of unusual strength of body and character."

Turner confesses that in his youth, living in the goldmine region of Australia, he was hot-blooded and reckless, and fell in with a gang of highway robbers, eventually becoming their leader. They attacked stations and convoys of gold-laden wagons. In one of those raids, all his companions were killed; only he and the wagon driver—McCarthy —survived. *"I wish to the Lord that I had shot him then, but I spared him,"* he says regretfully, because McCarthy was evil and devious, *"the devil incarnate."*

Then Turner moved to England and settled down to a quiet and respectable life, making up for the way in which the money had been earned. But McCarthy haunted and extorted him relentlessly for twenty years. The line was eventually crossed when McCarthy wanted Alice. Turner felt he had no choice. He was terminally ill and, in fact, he passed away seven months later. James, who in the meantime had gotten divorced, united with Alice, who knew nothing about the heavy shadow that burdened her father's life.

There is only one flaw in this otherwise excellent story. The dying McCarthy mutters something indistinct ending with the syllable *"rat."* In the context of the story, this single syllable has no meaning, but Sherlock Holmes manages to decipher the enigmatic significance of this word: it is the last syllable of the name Ballarat, the town in Australia where Turner came from. Thus, with his dying breath, McCarthy pronounced the word *Ballarat*, hoping that people would realize that his killer was from the Australian town of Ballarat.

Even the most intelligent and skillful reader cannot be expected to decode this obscure reference. It is simply outside the ken of any reader. After all, would it not be more logical for McCarthy to simply utter Turner's name before he expired? None of the *dramatis personae* in the story has ever heard of the Australian town of Ballarat, whereas Turner's name was familiar to one and all.

This minor flaw does not detract from the overall quality and accomplishments of the story.

SINISTER SECRETS UNEARTHED
THE STORY *THE ADVENTURE OF THE COPPER BEECHES*

Crime is common, logic is rare.
—Sherlock Holmes

A young woman named Violet Hunter seeks the advice and guidance of Sherlock Holmes. She is confused and conflicted as to what path to take. For the last five years, she served as a governess at the home of Colonel Spence Munro. When he was posted to Nova Scotia, Miss Hunter found herself jobless, her savings quickly diminishing and the bills accumulating.

She applies to a placement agency for governesses, hoping to land a position with adequate salary. She takes her place in a line of other young applicants. But when she enters the office, a stout, affable man with a smiling face is sitting next to the recruiting agent. As soon as Miss Hunter enters, the corpulent man jumps from his chair announcing, *"That will do... I could not ask for anything better. Capital! Capital."* All this before he has even heard a single word from the applicant and without checking her experience, recommendations, and suitability for the position. Even though her wage up to now has been four pounds a month, the jolly, chubby man offers her one hundred pounds a year. It is obvious, then, that it is neither her qualifications nor her experience that matter to the prospective employer, only her external appearance.

But why? What lies behind the generous offer that ignores professional qualifications and experience? Some further details are soon added to the offer. The smiling, stout man stipulates that the governess will have to don a certain dress and sit at a certain spot in the house, as instructed by her employers.

Miss Hunt is a little taken aback by the unusual demands, but is still inclined to accept the offer. However, the next request elicits a vehement refusal; she is required to cut her hair short before reporting for duty. Miss Hunt is particularly proud of her luxuriant chestnut-colored hair. But the cheerful, plump man—with a shadow now hovering over his face—is adamant, insisting that this is a non-negotiable condition. Miss Hunter rejects the offer. But when she goes back to her flat, she begins to doubt the wisdom of her decision to reject an extremely generous offer because of the quaint request to cut her hair short.

While she is weighing her options, a letter arrives from Mr. Jephro Rucastle, the stout and cheerful prospective employer. In it he repeats the offer and the essential condition about the hair, adding that the dress she is asked to wear belonged to his daughter Alice, who now lives in Philadelphia.

At this point, the reader can formulate the following theory:

It is clear that Miss Hunter was chosen for the position based solely on her appearance. The requirement that she occasionally put on Alice's dress suggests that she is supposed to impersonate Alice. The demand that she sit in a certain spot only corroborates this assumption. All this, apparently, is aimed at convincing someone observing from the outside, from a certain distance, that he is indeed watching Alice.

Naturally, several questions arise at this point: Who is that person that must be deluded into thinking that he is seeing Alice? What is his connection to Alice? If Alice is living in Philadelphia, why is he not told so explicitly and instead a young governess is hired to impersonate Alice? One wonders if Alice is indeed in Philadelphia. And if not, where is Alice? Is she dead? If she is, what is the purpose of creating the illusion that she is alive? Why is the fact of her death being withheld from that man?

If Alice is not dead, perhaps she has been kidnapped and is kept prisoner in a secret place. This last supposition is the most plausible, since it alone explains the need to create the illusion—through the impersonating governess—that Alice is alive and well. If Alice has been kidnapped and is confined somewhere against her will, what brought this about? Who could be interested in the abduction of a young woman? Is her presence so threatening to someone that he or she has resorted to such a drastic measure?

At this early stage of the unfolding story, these doubts and queries cannot be answered, but they certainly point the reader in the right direction. This is further substantiated by the fact that in his letter to Miss Hunter, Alice's father offers the governess the exorbitant sum of 120 pounds per year to come to his house in Winchester and take care of his six-year-old son (who, from his own father's description, sounds like a rather repulsive kid) and serve as Alice's double. Mr. Rucastle does not express it in so many words, but his intention is clear.

Sherlock Holmes takes a rather dim view of the proposal, "*I confess that it is not the situation which I should like to see a sister of mine apply for,*" he says. He is particularly suspicious of the request that Miss Hunter "*dress up*" as another person. As for the high remuneration, three times the going rate, Holmes is particularly skeptical.

Miss Hunter, however, despite Sherlock Holmes's reservations, decides to accept the offer, which is guaranteed to solve her financial problems.

The anticipated communication from Miss Hunter arrives not long after she assumes the position of governess in Winchester. The note says:

> *Please be at the Black Swan Hotel at Winchester*
> *at midday tomorrow. Do come! I am at my wit's*
> *end.*

Holmes and Watson immediately board a train to Winchester, and at the appointed hour, Miss Hunter waits for them at the Black Swan, agitated and baffled.

On their way to Winchester, they pass by pastoral scenes, with rolling hills and picturesque farmsteads. But Sherlock Holmes refuses to be beguiled by these enchanting landscapes:

> *They always fill me with a certain horror. It is my*
> *belief, Watson, founded upon my experience,*
> *that the lowest and vilest alleys in London do not*

present more dreadful record of sin than does
the smiling and beautiful countryside.

These impressions of Holmes function as a metaphor and as a proleptic hint, pointing us to the shabby, dilapidated house of Miss Hunter's new employers, which is surrounded by lovely woods and fields.

When they meet at the hotel, Miss Hunter tells Holmes and Watson about the strange events that have taken place since she began working for her new employers. Her mistress, Mrs. Rucastle, it turns out, is not mad; she is a silent, pale-faced woman, much younger than her husband (at least fifteen years) who was a widower when she married him. She leaves the management of the household entirely in her husband's hands. And yet, Miss Hunter reports, she seems to possess "*some secret sorrow.*"

Soon after her arrival, Miss Hunter is requested to wear an electric-blue dress, which bears the unmistakable signs of having been worn before. The dress fits Miss Hunter perfectly. Mr. Rucastle expresses exaggerated delight at the sight of the governess wearing the well-fitting dress.

Next she is requested to sit by a long window in the drawing room with her back to the window. This strange configuration conforms to the theory presented earlier: the person waiting for Alice must not see Miss Hunter's face, only her back, and assume that it is Alice who is sitting by the large window, alive, healthy, and in good cheer. In order to enhance and heighten this impression, Mr. Rucastle positions himself next to Miss Hunter, and tells her amusing anecdotes that make her laugh out loud. The man watching Alice will surely deduce that Alice is well and happy.

The spunky and curious Miss Hunter naturally wants to know what goes on behind her back, beyond the large window. Thus, the next time she is asked to put on the blue dress and position herself with her back to the window, she hides a piece of broken mirror in a handker-chief, and uses it to peek at the scene behind her. This is what she reports to Holmes and Watson:

> *At the second glance, however, I perceived that there was a man standing in the Southampton Road, a small bearded man in a grey suit, who seemed to be looking in my direction... This man, however, was leaning against the railing which boarded our field and was looking earnestly up.*

The hypothesis that Alice was abducted and is kept in captivity thus gains further substantiation. If the man (deceived by Miss Hunter's impersonation) assumes that Alice is alive and well in her father's house, why does he not call at the father's house, talk to her, reveal what is in his heart? There is only one possible answer: he knows that Alice's father will not let him in. The man is obviously wary and mistrustful.

Alice's father is well aware of the stranger's suspicions, so he instructs Miss Hunter, "Kindly turn around and wave him away, like that."

This gesture of dismissal is meant to convey to Alice's admirer that she no longer wants his attention.

Mr. Rucastle warns Alice not to walk in the garden after dark because that is when a fearsome mastiff is let loose and roams the grounds hungry and growling. This may explain why the man enamored of Alice cannot come any closer (not knowing, however, that she is being impersonated by Miss Hunter).

Miss Hunter further recounts a very bizarre incident that happened to her. With some ingenuity, she managed to open a locked drawer in an old chest of drawers found in her room. To her utter amazement, it contained a coil of hair very similar to her own coil of hair, which she had kept at the bottom of her trunk. Clearly, this hair hidden in the drawer must be Alice's hair, cut for some unexplained reason. This is why Alice's impersonator, who has very similar hair, was required to sacrifice her own hair in order to resemble the kidnapped Alice and to drive away the unknown suitor.

This is the part where the detective part of the story ends, the part that exposes the mystery and helps the reader solve it even before Sherlock Holmes does. Here the analytical-theoretical part of the investigation ends and the practical, actual detective part begins: the collection of evidence and the examination of the findings, which will corroborate the results of the analytical-theoretical investigation. In fact, it is the appropriately named Miss Hunter who starts the practical investigation. She notices that one wing of the house is uninhabited and always dark. One day, while climbing the stairs to the shuttered section of the house, she comes across Mr. Rucastle exiting a door, which was always kept locked.

> *One day, however, as I ascended the stair, I met*
> *Mr. Rucastle coming out through this door, his*
> *keys in his hand, and a look on his face which*
> *made him a very different person to the round,*
> *jovial man to whom I was accustomed. His*
> *cheeks were red, his brow was all crinkled with*
> *anger, and the veins stood out at his temples*
> *with passion, He locked the door and hurried*
> *past me without a word or a look.*

In an attempt to conceal what can no longer be a secret, Mr. Rucastle apologizes to Miss Hunter for not greeting her earlier, explaining that he was preoccupied with business matters. As for the locked room, he claims that he uses it as a dark room where he develops his films, as photography is one of his hobbies. Then he adds:

> *'But, dear me! What an observant young lady we*
> *have come upon. Who would have believed it?*
> *Who would have ever believed it!' He spoke in a*
> *jesting tone, but there was no jest in his eyes as*
> *he looked at me. I read suspicion there and*
> *annoyance but no jest.*

The hypothesis that Alice has been abducted (by her father, though we are not sure as yet) and is kept in the dark room gains further corroboration, as Miss Hunter further tells Holmes and Watson:

> *I may tell you that besides Mr. Rucastle, both*
> *Toller and his wife find something to do in these*

deserted rooms, and I once saw him carrying a
large black linen bag with him through the door.

The courageous and resourceful Miss Hunter is determined to solve the mystery of the locked door. She sees an
opportunity when Toller, the servant, drunk more than
usual, has left the key in the door of the locked room. She
enters the dark room only to realize that it leads to a series
of other rooms, all empty, dusty, and cheerless. Once
again she finds herself facing a locked door. She hears
steps inside the room and sees a shadow pass against the
dim light coming from the slit under the door. In a panic,
she rushes down the passage and straight into the arms of
Mr. Rucastle, who has been waiting for her there. He is
still smiling but his voice is menacing:

> "*[The door is locked] 'to keep people out who*
> *have no business there. Do you see?' He was*
> *still smiling in the most amiable manner... 'And if*
> *you ever put your foot over that threshold*
> *again—' Here in an instant the smile hardened*
> *into a grin of rage, and he glared down at me*
> *with a face of a demon—'I'll throw you to the*
> *mastiff.'*

Thus ends Miss Hunter's report to Holmes and Watson.
The young woman is still shaken by all that has happened
to her. There is mounting evidence that Miss Hunter was
hired for the sole purpose of impersonating Alice—
kidnapped and imprisoned in order to drive away a prospective suitor—pretending that she is alive and well and

happy with her lot. It is evident now that Alice's father, the corpulent, jolly, smiling, but evil, Mr. Rucastle, has locked his daughter up in a remote, dark room in the house. The reason for this, the last component of the puzzle, is not yet known.

At this point in the narrative, Holmes sums up what the reader already knows:

> *"You [Miss Hunter" have been brought there to personate someone, and the real person is imprisoned in this chamber. That is obvious. As to who this person is, I have no doubt that it is the daughter, Miss Alice Rucasle, if I remember right, who was said to have gone to America. You were chosen, doubtless, as resembling her in height, figure and the color of your hair. Hers had been cut off, very possibly in some illness through which she has passed, and so, of course, yours had to be sacrificed also. By a curious chance you came upon her tresses. The man in the road was undoubtedly some friend of hers—possibly her fiancé—and no doubt, as you wore the girl's dress and were so like her, he was convinced from your laughter, whenever he saw you, and afterwards from your gesture, that Miss Rucastle was perfectly happy, and that she no longer desires his attentions. The dog is let loose at night to prevent him from endeavoring to communicate with her.*

I hate to break it to you, Mr. Holmes, but the intelligent, perceptive reader has already reached all your conclusions, starting with the first encounter between Miss Hunter and Mr. Rucastle, when he hired her as a governess solely on the basis of her looks, not her qualifications, and made the offer contingent on her assuming someone else's personality, all for a very generous compensation. The reader is fully aware of all this before Holmes's analysis.

Next, Sherlock Holmes and Dr. Watson initiate a nocturnal meeting with Mr. Rucastle. The latter lets loose the famished mastiff, but to everyone's horror, the beast attacks Mr. Rucastle himself, sinking its fangs in his neck. Dr. Watson shoots the dog, saving Mr. Rucastle's life, but the accident leaves him disabled for the rest of his life. The housekeeper, Mrs. Toller, now supplies the missing information that ties up all the loose ends and brings about the resolution.

Following the death of Alice's mother and the father's marriage to a much younger woman, the daughter was under pressure to sign over her share of her mother's inheritance to her father. Alice adamantly refused to comply. When Mr. Fowler, a prospective suitor for Alice's hand appeared on the scene, the greedy father suspected that a husband would object to such embezzlement of the young woman's funds and would do his best to foil it.

But all's well that ends well. Mr. Rucastle remained a broken man, kept alive through the care of his devoted wife. Alice recovered, married Mr. Fowler, and moved to the island of Mauritius where her husband held a government appointment.

Only Dr. Watson is disappointed at the end; he has noticed that Sherlock Holmes was quite taken by the clever, resourceful, and courageous Miss Hunter. But as soon as the case is solved and she ceases to be at the center of one of his problems, Holmes manifests no further interest in her.

SIX EQUAL ONE
THE STORY *THE ADVENTURE OF THE SIX NAPOLEONS*

The story opens with a seemingly minor, yet bizarre, crime. Someone has broken into the residence of Dr. Barnicot, an enthusiastic admirer of Napoleon. The house is full of books, pictures, and relics of the French emperor. However, the burglar took only one item: a plaster bust of Napoleon. And he did not take it with him; he carried it outside, and smashed it savagely against the garden wall. The doctor realized what had happened only the following day. When he reached his clinic, he was surprised to find that the window had been opened during the night and pieces of his second Napoleon bust were strewn all over the room.

Inspector Lastrade, the famous (or infamous) Scotland Yard official, theorizes that the perpetrator must be a mentally unhinged person. In keeping with the conventions of the Sherlock Holmes genre, the police inspector's version will eventually prove unfounded and absurd.

Dr. Watson, too, surmises that the perpetrator must be someone who has an *idee fixe*, an obsession with Napoleon. This is not a very illuminating opinion. Watson is not stupid, of course, but he has a mediocre intellect and limited imagination, thus serving as a foil to Sherlock Holmes and underlining the latter's genius.

The savvy, intelligent reader, on the other hand, can already form a certain theory: first, the claim of mental illness should be discounted; both cases (as well as the cases that come to light later) show a distinct pattern and a method, both atypical of a mentally disturbed person. The theory of an *idee fixe* is equally specious: London is replete with sculptures and images of the Emperor Napoleon, displayed openly in parks and public squares. Why does the obsessive person not attack those images and break them to smithereens?

Thus, the preliminary theory can claim only this: the unknown burglar is interested only in busts of Napoleon. He does not steal nor does he deface any other object, not even pictures and relics of the emperor. He smashes those busts outside, under a street lamp, where there is light. What is he looking for among the broken pieces of the busts? Is it something valuable, worth the risk of being caught in a burglary? Is it a diamond? A precious stone? And how does the burglar know where to find those busts?

There are hundreds of Napoleon busts around London and in the country. Can he possibly steal and smash all of them? That does not stand to reason. It is, therefore, safe to assume that the unknown criminal knows that only a few busts actually contain the valuable object that he is after. How does he know where those particular busts are located? At the moment we have no answer to this question. It is clear, however, that someone—perhaps the burglar himself—hid a valuable object inside one of the busts, presumably while the bust was still wet and soft and malleable.

As we see later, this inchoate theory, which is at the disposal of the intelligent, keen reader, in fact, covers most of the solution. What we need now are some more details to fill in the outline of the preliminary theory.

The third burglary occurs soon after the first two. This time the crime involves murder. The murder takes place at the home of Mr. Harker, a journalist, who is frightened and severely shaken by the incident. But above all, Mr. Harker bemoans the fact that he is unable to report on such a momentous event that happened right at his doorstep.

Once again, a house has been broken into. Again, a bust of Napoleon has been stolen and smashed into pieces. But this time the criminal left a murder victim on the scene, whose identity has not yet been discovered. This time, too, the bust was shattered in a well-lighted place, which strengthens the theory that the perpetrator was looking for something specific in the pieces of the broken bust.

The police find a photograph of a singularly ugly man in a pocket of the murdered man's garment:

> *...alert, sharp-featured, simian man, with thick eyebrows and a very peculiar projection of the lower part of the face, like the muzzle of a baboon.*

Sherlock Holmes and Dr. Watson pay a visit to a workshop where the plaster busts were made. The owner of the workshop recognizes the ill-favored man in the photograph: an Italian worker named Beppo.

Next, the two visit the manager of the store that sold those busts, and he confirms that he has indeed sold six busts of Napoleon. The sight of Beppo's pictures elicits a furious reaction from him. The man, he claims, is a rascal. He was accused of attempted murder, having knifed a fellow Italian. He was sentenced to a year in jail.

When Holmes confers with Inspector Lastrade, the latter brags that his methods are superior to those of Holmes, who vainly chases after Napoleon's busts while he, Lastrade, has already succeeded in identifying the dead man and the cause of the crime. The victim is Pietro Venucci, from Naples, a notorious Mafioso. The irony is that knowing the victim's identity does not advance the main investigation, which tracks the shattered plaster busts.

That night, pursuing Holmes's line of investigation, he and Watson go to Laburnum Villa, where they crouch in the shade by the fence. Before long, they see a *"lithe, dark figure, as swift and active as an ape"*, rushing up the garden path. The description fits Beppo, who now breaks into the villa to steal another Napoleonic bust. Holmes, Watson, and Lestrade—who has joined them—together overpower the criminal.

It turns out that in the meantime, Holmes has identified and located the owner of the sixth bust, who is, of course, ignorant of the significance of the object in his possession. Sherlock Holmes has invited Watson and Lastrade to his apartment, and together, they await the arrival of the man from Reading. In a formal, ceremonious fashion, Holmes pays him the exorbitant sum of ten pounds for the sixth Napoleonic bust.

And now Holmes reaches the climax of his theatrical presentation: while Watson and Lastrade watch expectantly, Holmes places the bust on a clean white cloth atop the table. Picking his hunting crop, he strikes Napoleon a sharp blow on the top of the head, breaking the figure into fragments. With a loud shout of triumph, Holmes then extracts from a splinter of the bust a round dark shining object. It is the famous black pearl of the Borgias.

The stunned Watson and Lastrade clap their hands. Holmes reconstructs the history of the black pearl and explains how it ended up inside the sixth bust of Napoleon. This reconstruction corresponds to the initial theory conceived by the perceptive intelligent reader. Holmes's line of inquiry was based on three phases: first, he located the workshop where the busts were molded and manufactured; second, he identified the merchants who bought the six Napoleons from the workshop; third, he located the people who had bought the busts.

And this is the trajectory of the black pearl: Pietro Venucci, an Italian crook, managed to steal the precious jewel from the hotel room of the prince who owned it, presumably with the help of his cousin Lucretia Venucci, who was employed as a maid there. Beppo then stole the pearl from Pietro Venucci. But while the pearl was in his possession, the police were on his trail for some minor crime he had committed. He was working at the factory where plaster statuettes were manufactured and a few minutes before the police caught up with him, he noticed the six newly minted busts standing on a shelf. He made a hole in one of them and hid the unique pearl inside. He was duly arrested by the police, and sentenced to a year in prison.

Upon his release, he began searching for the bust with the precious stone. With the help of collaborators, he managed to obtain the names and addresses of the people who had purchased the busts. One by one, he broke into their houses, took the Napoleonic busts and broke them to pieces, hoping to find the black pearl inside. On the third break-in, at the house of the journalist, he was followed by Pietro Venucci, the original purloiner of the pearl. In the fight that ensued, Beppo murdered his pursuer.

Beppo broke into five houses and stole five busts, but none of them contained the black pearl. Sherlock Holmes was able to locate the sixth owner, invited him to his house, and in the presence of Dr. Watson and Inspector Lestrade, he bought the sixth bust from its owner, then in a dramatic gesture, smashed it to smithereens. While Watson and Lestrade watched in utter amazement, Holmes extracted the inimitable precious jewel from one of the shards.

Holmes's hypothesis that something of great value is buried inside one of the busts was already shared by the reader. All that was needed was to fill in the details.

This story is a classic example of a detective story where an intelligent, sensitive reader is given a fair chance to identify and reconstruct the mystery, even before Sherlock Holmes himself formulates the hypothesis.

NO USE LYING
THE STORY *THE ADVENTURE OF ABBEY GRANGE*

Sherlock Holmes—as always, accompanied by Dr. Watson—is summoned by Stanley Hopkins, a local police inspector, to Abbey Grange, a stately home in Kent. It is reported that three burglars, an older man and two younger ones, presumably his sons, broke into the house. The owner of the estate, Sir Eustace Brackenstall, surprised them in the act and they killed him. His young, graceful wife was bound to a chair and gagged. Somehow, the wife was able to remove the handkerchief from her mouth and called for help. This is the sum of the wife's first report to Sherlock Holmes.

It is Dr. Watson's keen eye that spots the first crack in the exquisite woman's account:

> *The lady lay back exhausted upon a couch, but her quick, observant gaze as we entered the room, and the alert expression of her beautiful features showed that neither her wits nor her courage had been shaken by her terrible experience.*

Indeed, one wonders how a young, delicate woman, who has just witnessed the murder of her husband, can be so poised and restrained. She describes how her husband

---

surprised the three burglars, how they bound her to a chair with a bell rope, how they stopped her mouth, and how they murdered her husband in front of her very eyes.

Another question arises. Since she saw the criminals and was able to identify them, why did they not kill her as well? This is another query that her version of events raises.

In addition, we are told that the husband was a notorious drunkard who used to torment and abuse his wife. This may explain why she does not mourn his departure. Dr. Watson seems to accept that this may be the reason why she did not evince much shock after the horrible incident. This is hard to accept, though, since a brutal murder perpetrated by three thugs in the middle of the night—while the witness is bound and gagged—is bound to affect that witness profoundly. But Dr. Watson notes that the woman does not seem shaken by the events, and this immediately throws some doubt on the veracity of her version of events.

The woman continues her testimony:

> When I opened my eyes I found that they had collected the silver from the sideboard, and they had drawn a bottle of wine which stood there. Each of them had a glass in his hand.

This testimony raises two questions. First, does it stand to reason that three robbers, who had just murdered the master of the house, would be content with such a meager loot of only a few silver pieces? And second, having just committed a heinous crime, wouldn't they try to flee the scene of the crime as soon as possible? Instead, the lady reports that they sat around comfortably and sipped wine.

At this point, a sensible, perceptive reader—even without any help from Sherlock Holmes—smells a rat; surely, the lady is not telling the truth. This conclusion gains further proof by the maid's testimony. Theresa Wright, who has been with her mistress since the latter's early childhood in Australia, defends her mistress's fabrication with lies of her own:

> *As I sat by my bedroom window, I saw three*
> *men in the moonlight down by the lodge gate*
> *yonder, but I thought nothing of it at the time.*

Indeed! A five-year-old would find a better excuse. Three men invade the estate in the dead of night, approach the main door, and the maid watches them calmly, never imagining that there may be something wrong with this picture.

Holmes is compelled to comment: *"Surely there are details in her story which, if we looked at it in cold blood would excite our suspicion."* And earlier he notes, *"The lady's charming personality must not be permitted to warp our judgment."* And even more explicitly:

> *... Lady Brackenstall and her maid have deliber-*
> *ately lied to us, that not one word of their story is*
> *to be believed...*

Sherlock Holmes then reaches the same conclusion that the perceptive reader has already reached.

After carefully examining the scene of the crime, Holmes comes to the conclusion that not three men, but only one man—a man of impressive proportions—committed the murder. Who is that man? Did the lady and her maid lie to protect him? If so, what is the connection between him and the lady? Here, as is often the case, Holmes keeps the cards close to his chest, conceals information, and blocks the reader (and Dr. Watson as well) from obtaining it.

In a manner that remains unknown to both the reader and Dr. Watson, Sherlock Holmes has located an Australian captain named Crocker, who used to be first officer on the *Rock of Gibraltar*, the ship that brought the lady (then a single girl named Mary Fraser) from Australia to England. The first officer fell head over heels in love with the beautiful, graceful girl. Soon afterward, however, she married a rich English aristocrat. Crocker continued to sail the seas and eventually became a captain.

Holmes located Crocker in the dockyard and invited him to his Baker Street apartment. The young captain, tall, muscular, and suntanned, showed up at the appointed time and frankly and candidly told Holmes and Watson his story.

It turns out that while waiting for his new assignment, he happened to run into the maid, Theresa Wright, and she told him about the abuse her mistress was suffering at the hands of her drunken husband. This drove him mad. The previous night, when the captain came secretly to see his beloved, the husband, awakened by the noise, rushed liked a madman into the room, reviled his wife, and welted her across the face with a stick. Crocker grabbed hold of a poker and killed him.

Holmes decides that this is an extraordinary case that can be construed as self-defense rather than murder. Thus, he does not turn the captain in, but instead sends him on his way, advising him to come back in a year's time and be reunited with his beloved.

Another Sherlock Holmes mystery has come to an end. At the start, the reader was allowed to participate in the detection process, but later on, Holmes blocked the channel of information, reserving it to himself so he alone could solve the mystery and reap the glory.

THE FATHER, THE SON, AND THE UNHOLY SPIRIT
THE STORY *THE REIGATE PUZZLE*

Dr. Watson and Sherlock Holmes are vacationing in the country house of Colonel Hayter, an old friend of Dr. Watson from his military service in Afghanistan. Holmes is in dire need of rest and recuperation after a couple of months of grueling international investigation that left him mentally exhausted.

After dinner, the three men lounge in the sunroom. When it is time to retire, the colonel remarks that he is taking a pistol with him *"in case we have an alarm."* He explains that lately there has been a break-in at the house of Old Acton. It was a rather peculiar burglary:

> *The thieves ransacked the library and got very little for their pains. The place was turned upside down, drawers burst open, and presses ransacked, with the result that an odd volume of Pope's 'Homer,' two plated candlesticks, an ivory letter-weight, a small oak barometer, and a ball of twine are all that have vanished."*

Two things are immediately clear. First, it is obvious that the burglars are rank amateurs. They picked up indiscriminate objects in order to stage a burglary because they could not find the object that they were looking for. They ransacked the library not because they were after a book but because they were looking for a certain document. This is borne out by the fact that they turned the place upside down and emptied drawers. Evidently, they did not find the document they were after, so before leaving, they faked a burglary, grabbing hold of anything they could get. Professional burglars are not local people; they come from afar, break in, take their booty, and disappear from the area. Amateur burglars, on the other hand, must be local fellows.

Who could break into Mr. Acton's house looking for a specific document? There is only one logical answer: Mr. Cunnigham and his son Alec. Colonel Hayter tells his guests about a legal dispute between the Cunninghams and Mr. Acton:

> Old Acton has some claim on half of Cunning-
> ham's estate, and the lawyers have been at it
> with both hands.

Thus, the father and son had a motive to break into Mr. Acton's house to look for a document that could support his claim against them.

Soon afterwards, another burglary takes place, this time at the Cunnigham estate. Since the first break-in was so unprofessional, it could be reasonably assumed that the second break-in would be equally amateurish, but this time, there is a difference: it involves murder. The victim is William Kirwan, the Cunninghams' coachman.

Alec Cunningham testifies that he was awakened at midnight and witnessed the struggle between the intruder and the coachman; he heard the shot, and then saw the fellow flee the scene toward the road.

However, an interesting piece of evidence surfaces: a small piece of torn paper was stuck between the finger and thumb of the dead man. It bears the inscription:

...at quarter to twelve...learn what... may...

Even the police inspector, who often blunders and utters specious assertions, declares with certainly that the truncated message points to an appointment at a quarter to midnight. But who could have summoned the coachman to such a nocturnal appointment? Who wrote that note? One thing becomes clear: the note was written by two different persons. This is deduced from variations in the handwriting. The words "learn" and "what" were written by a weaker, less assertive hand, while the word "quarter" is squeezed between the words "at" and "to" suggesting that it was written afterwards.

Thus, we have one note produced by two different writers: the more assertive script belongs to a young person, while the hesitant script to an older person. The connection to the Cunninghams, father and son, immediately suggests itself. But why do they write the note jointly? Perhaps there is something incriminating about the father and son and they do not trust each other. What is it that implicates these two?

Coachman William Kirwan was invited to an appointment at midnight in order to eliminate him, presumably because he knew about the burglary at Mr. Acton's house. This suspicion cannot yet be verified but it is a logical assumption.

Note that all these observations are presented and identified before Sherlock Holmes puts them forth. *The Reigate Puzzle* is a classic example where an astute and alert reader can analyze the facts laid out in the text, and with method and logic can arrive at a solution to the mystery. Certainly, further on in the story, Holmes presents the same analyses and reaches the same conclusions. He does this displaying his usual dramatic, theatrical strategies.

In the pocket of Alec Cunningham's dressing gown, Holmes finds the incriminating note written jointly by father and son. As is his wont, he keeps the cards close to his chest and does not divulge all the information that may lead the reader to the solution. Thus, for instance, it is only at the last minute that Holmes explains that Alec Cunningham's claim, that the unknown burglar shot the coachman while the two men were wrestling, is baseless because there was no gunpowder residue on the victim's clothes, suggesting that the shot came from a distance of more than four yards.

Similarly, Holmes disproves both father and son's claim that they saw the burglar escape into the road. There were no boot marks on the side of the moist ditch that the burglar supposedly crossed, proving once more that the Cunningham's version was a fabrication.

These late observations serve to corroborate the conclusions already reached by the reader.

Sherlock Holmes maintains his supremacy while the reader gets a fair chance at solving the puzzle.

EVEN A MAESTRO
CAN MAKE A MISTAKE
The Story *The Adventure of the Empty House*

There is no doubt that *The Adventure of the Empty House* is riddled with flaws and is sloppily written from a thematic, as well as a compositional perspective. The story gives the impression of being an arbitrary amalgam of disconnected plots and episodes.

I have chosen to analyze this particular story on purpose, in order to present a Sherlock Holmes story that is not one of the master's best.

The story opens with the unexpected death—murder—of the Honorable Ronald Adair.

Until his sudden death, the life of this young man was pleasant and uneventful: he had no enemies and no particular vices. However, he was very fond of playing cards. He might have lost five pounds at a game, but not much more. On the last day of his life, he played in partnership with Colonel Moran, and the two had won 420 pounds. It is, therefore, strange that after such enormous win, Adair was murdered. Could it be that Colonel Moran shot his young partner to get hold of his half of the considerable winning?

Theoretically, this is possible, but it turns out that the door of Adair's room was locked from the inside. There were no signs of anyone entering through the window (such as footprints, trampled flowerbeds, scratches on the windowsill, etc.). The only possible theoretical explanation could be a gunshot through the window. However, it was impossible to figure out how anyone could shoot from such a distance.

The narrator—Dr. Watson, now by himself after the death of Sherlock Holmes at the hand of his archenemy Professor Moriarty—does not pursue the theory that Colonel Moran found a way to kill Ronald Adair. Instead, he focuses on an episode that has nothing to do with the murder of Adair. There is no obvious link between what happens next and the initial plot, which makes the story look like patchwork.

In the street, Watson bumps up against an elderly, deformed man and knocks down several books the man is carrying. Watson picks up the books and apologizes. The man hastens to disappear. To Watson's surprise, soon afterwards, the old man shows up in Dr. Watson's apartment and thanks him for his help. It is clear that the situation is not to Watson's liking. Watson turns his head to look at his bookshelf (the old man, who is a bookseller, tries to sell Watson some books), and when he turns back, to his utter amazement, he sees Sherlock Holmes standing in front of him, smiling. This is after three years that the detective has been considered dead. The shock causes Watson to faint, and Holmes restores him to consciousness with a shot of brandy.

Holmes apologizes for having disappeared for three years and for maintaining the illusion that both he and Professor Moriarty died in the waterfall in Switzerland. It turns out that Holmes was able to save himself from

Professor Moriarty's murderous clutches, and that it was only the professor who died in the waterfall. Holmes describes in great detail the mortal struggle and his courageous escape from Professor Moriarty's confederate, Colonel Moran. That name was mentioned earlier, in connection with Roland Adair's murder, as a potential suspect. Since several other henchmen of Professor Moriarty were pursuing Holmes, he had to flee and seek refuge in faraway places, such as Tibet, Persia, Mecca, Khartoum and, eventually, France.

Now that Holmes is again installed in his rooms in Baker Street (which were kept intact for him for three years), he invites Dr. Watson to go on a nocturnal adventure.

Holmes leads Dr. Watson along the dark back alleys, mews, stables, and narrow passages of London until they come to a deserted house. When Watson looks through a dim window he realizes, to his great surprise, that they are facing Holmes's apartment on Baker Street. Moreover, inside the apartment he recognizes the figure of none other than Sherlock Holmes himself.

Holmes explains to the amazed Watson that a French artist has fashioned a wax molding of him, and now the effigy is dressed in Holmes's habitual dressing gown. This ruse will later fool his enemies into thinking that he is at home. Inspector Lestrade joins Holmes and Watson while two constables patrol the street outside. The men maintain total silence and are enveloped in darkness as they watch the street.

Suddenly they hear the stealthy sound of footsteps and see a shadowy figure creeping menacingly into the room.

Holmes and Watson overpower the man as soon as he has fired his specialized air gun at the figure across the street. The man turns out to be Colonel Moran, the same man who tried to kill Holmes at the Reichenbach Falls in Switzerland.

Colonel Sebastian Moran had a distinguished military career in India, but after retiring from the army, he came to London, where he *"acquired an evil name,"* and was soon recruited by Professor Moriarty, who used him mostly for special, high-class jobs. Falling for Holmes's ploy, he took the waxen image to be the real Sherlock Holmes and shot it with his *"soft revolver."*

Holmes surmises that Colonel Moran shot the Honorable Ronald Adair because he suspected that the young man had discovered that the colonel was cheating at cards, which may also explain their big win. This conjecture is not very convincing, given that Colonel Moran had already gotten his share of the loot. A more cogent explanation could be that the greedy colonel wanted young Adair's share as well.

Either way, the story opens and ends with the murder of Ronald Adair, which creates an impression of a complete circle, or at least a partial one. But, as noted earlier, as far as composition, theme, structure, and plot are concerned the story exhibits some serious faults and errors. It is a hodge-podge of disparate elements lumped together rather arbitrarily. There is no real link between the murder of Ronald Adair and the (overly) detailed description of the struggle between Holmes and Professor Moriarty by the waterfall in Switzerland. There is no organic connection between the book merchant episode and the attempt on Holmes's life by Colonel Moran.

Indeed, there are no structural links between all these unrelated elements of the plot. Perhaps the story can be compared to a mine whence raw material for other stories might be extracted. But until then, one can only conclude that even a maestro can make mistakes.

ABOUT THE AUTHOR

Dr. Yair Mazor is Professor Emeritus of modern Hebrew literature and biblical literature with the University Wisconsin–Milwaukee.

He is the author of 28 books and over 250 articles and critical reviews. Dr. Mazor's fields of study are modern Hebrew literature, Enlightenment Hebrew literature in the 19th century in Eastern Europe, biblical literature, comparative literature, Scandinavian literature, and Hebrew children's literature.

Dr. Mazor has earned numerous scholarly awards, among them the Shpam Prize and Dov Sadan Prize from the University of Tel Aviv for two of his books; the Baron Prize for exceptional excellence in research in the field of Jewish Studies; the "Distinguished Undergraduate Teaching Award" from the University of Wisconsin–Milwaukee; and a national award, the "Most Distinguished Scholar of Hebrew Studies in the USA, the Friedman Prize.

In his military service, Dr. Mazor acted as a combat paratrooper, as well as an instructor of parachuting.

www.ingramcontent.com/pod-product-compliance
Lightning Source LLC
Chambersburg PA
CBHW060436090426

42733CB00011B/2299